# ENDORSEMENTS

Many books have been written on this subject. This is the *only* one that shows you *how!*

SID ROTH
Host, *It's Supernatural!* Television

Whether you are a brand-new convert or not even a convert yet—or you have been in ministry for years—the chances are very strong that there are things holding you back from fulfilling your heavenly assignments. *Live Free* is a book that will walk you through the steps to freedom.

WILLIAM J. MORFORD, Shalom Ministries
Author/translator of *The One New Man Bible*

# LIVE
## FREE

# LIVE
## *FREE*

DISCOVER THE KEYS TO
LIVING IN GOD'S PRESENCE 24/7

DENNIS & DR. JEN CLARK

NOTE: To protect the privacy of individuals in testimonies and true stories, we have given them fictitious names.

DESTINY IMAGE® PUBLISHERS, INC.

P.O. Box 310, Shippensburg, PA 17257-0310

*"Promoting Inspired Lives."*

This book and all other Destiny Image, Revival Press, MercyPlace, Fresh Bread, Destiny Image Fiction, and Treasure House books are available at Christian bookstores and distributors worldwide.

For a U.S. bookstore nearest you, call 1-800-722-6774.

For more information on foreign distributors, call 717-532-3040.

Reach us on the Internet: www.destinyimage.com.

ISBN 13 TP: 978-0-7684-4241-0

ISBN 13 Ebook: 978-0-7684-8464-9

For Worldwide Distribution, Printed in the U.S.A.

1 2 3 4 5 6 7 8 / 17 16 15 14 13

# DEDICATION

We dedicate this book to Molly U. Tarr

Thank you, Molly, for your encouragement, enthusiasm, suggestions, and support.

You have been our dear friend, intercessor, and sounding board throughout the years.

*We use our powerful God-tools for...fitting every loose thought and emotion and impulse into the structure of life shaped by Christ.*
—2 Corinthians 10:4-5 MSG

# CONTENTS

Preface . . . . . . . . . . . . . . . . . . . . . . . . . . . . . . . 15

Introduction . . . . . . . . . . . . . . . . . . . . . . . . . 17

Chapter 1    Touching God . . . . . . . . . . . . . . . . . . . . . . . 25

Chapter 2    Our Stories . . . . . . . . . . . . . . . . . . . . . . . . 39

Chapter 3    The Power of Testimonies . . . . . . . . . . . . . . 51

Chapter 4    God-Tools . . . . . . . . . . . . . . . . . . . . . . . . . 61

Chapter 5    Location, Location, Location . . . . . . . . . . . 77

Chapter 6    Dropping Down . . . . . . . . . . . . . . . . . . . . . 89

Chapter 7    The Grace of Yielding . . . . . . . . . . . . . . . . 101

Chapter 8    The Peace of God . . . . . . . . . . . . . . . . . . . . 111

Interlude    Communion Without Ceasing
             under The Peace of God . . . . . . . . . . . . . . . 125

Chapter 9    Forgive 1-2-3 . . . . . . . . . . . . . . . . . . . . . . . 131

Chapter 10   Stay Connected 24/7 . . . . . . . . . . . . . . . . . 143

# PREFACE

Dear Reader,

This is a personal letter written to you. I was the first one to embark on this journey with Dennis as my mentor, and it was just the beginning of what has been the most exciting and fulfilling time of my life. I could tell you many stories, but *I am* the story!

I am grateful to Dennis for being my husband, my best friend, my pastor, and my mentor. What I learned from him and put into practice in my life has led to an *Extreme Makeover: Jen Edition*. The fruit of this extraordinary transformation has manifested in heart healing, spiritual and physical health, a closer relationship with God, and a new-found purpose in life. I can hardly even remember the pains and fears that were once my constant companions. My testimony can become your story too.

What you will learn in the pages of this book were first proven in my own life; but in the past decades these keys have worked for thousands of other people as well. In fact, this process works for everyone who wants it—no exceptions! I guarantee that if you will put what you read into practice, you will have grown by the time you're finished reading this book. Though maturity is never instantaneous, what is contained here will transform you so completely that people may not even recognize you when you're done.

The learning scale is quick. And I can personally testify that it really works.

Blessings,

DR. JEN CLARK

# INTRODUCTION

## THE SPIRITUAL REALM

God wants to be the Lord of our entire life, not just our "spiritual" life. Since God made each one of us as thinking, willing, and feeling beings, He wants us to allow Him to be Lord of our thoughts, choices, and emotions. Throughout the Bible we're told God's thoughts are higher than our thoughts (see Isa. 55:8-9; Rom. 11:33-34), His will is preferable to the choices we would make on our own (see Prov. 14:12; 3:5-7), and His love is superior to our carnal emotions and desires (see 1 Cor. 13; 1 John 2:15-17).

Jesus said, *"God is spirit, and those who worship Him must worship in spirit and truth"* (John 4:24). Jesus not only tells us that God is a Spirit, but that He is also known and worshiped through the spirit—our human spirit. In other words, a spiritual God communicates with humans in the realm of the spirit. There is no other way to know God than by the Spirit of God revealing Himself to our human spirits. This is why Paul writes to the Corinthians, reminding them:

> *But God has revealed them to us through His Spirit. For the Spirit searches all things, yes, the deep things of God. For what man knows the things of a man except the spirit of the man which is in him? Even so no one knows the things of God except the Spirit of God. Now we have received, not the spirit of the world, but the Spirit who is from God, that we might know the things that have been freely given to us by God* (1 Corinthians 2:10-12).

## SPIRIT, SOUL, AND BODY

The word *spirit* is used more than 900 times throughout the Scriptures, referring to God, angels, and demons. But it also refers to our human spirit as well. God is a Spirit, yes; and since He created man in His image, we are spirit beings as well (see Gen. 1:26-28). Adam and Eve had spirits that communed with God, their spirit touching the Spirit of God.

Paul reveals that humans have a body, a soul, and a spirit (see 1 Thess. 5:23). Physically, with his body, Adam could feel the breeze blow and touch the plants placed in the garden. Adam also had the ability to think and make choices—God let him choose the names of all of the animals that were created (see Gen. 2:18-20). And Adam also had emotions—he loved God and He felt God's love toward him.

Some theologians argue about what the soul is, or what the spirit of man is, and whether or not it is correct to make a distinction between the two. But what everyone agrees on, however, is that God created man to be a thinking, willing, feeling being; and all three of these faculties should be under the influence of God. Adam, like us, was formed as a spirit, living in a material body, possessing a mind, will, and emotions—or what is called the soul of man.

## EMOTIONAL GOD

The Bible reveals that God has emotions—He gives and receives love, He laughs and cries, He is happy and angry, etc. He not only has emotions, but His very nature is emotion. John writes, *"God is love, and he who abides in love abides in God, and God in him"* (1 John 4:16). God does not simply possess love, but He is love.

The entire atmosphere of the Garden of Eden was permeated with the love, joy, and peace of God—the supernatural emotions of God. It wasn't just a theory that was to be mentally known, but a present reality that Adam and Eve experienced continually. Adam and Eve actually felt the love, joy, and peace of God every moment of every day. They walked in perfect harmony with Him.

## PERFECT HARMONY

Before Adam and Eve sinned, they were in perfect harmony with God's thoughts, will, and emotions. In fact, emotions were created to be transmitters of God's supernatural emotions; also thoughts should be transmitters of God's thoughts, and the will a transmitter of God's will. But once sin entered the world, their spirits were separated from God—they died a spiritual death in the very moment they ate of the fruit of the tree of knowledge of good and evil. Harmony between God and man was suddenly fractured. Adam and Eve became ruled by the flesh rather than by their spirit. Their fallen nature and God's heavenly nature no longer matched.

Even though they enjoyed perfect fellowship with God before sin, now Adam and Eve had some bad ideas about Him. They suddenly felt the need to run from God when He came around to talk with them. They also made some bad choices. To their dismay, Adam began to feel unpleasant emotions like hurt and anger that Eve had gotten them into this mess, which was all mixed up with guilt, shame, and fear. Their thoughts, choices, and emotions—their souls—were now under the influence of the law of sin and death.

## SPIRITUAL REBIRTH

But through spiritual rebirth we can now be reconnected with God. Jesus died on the cross to pay the penalty for the sins of mankind through the shedding of His own blood. He *"made peace through the blood of His cross"* (Col. 1:20). Because of Jesus's death, burial, and resurrection, man can now experience spiritual rebirth and enjoy perfect communion with God once again.

Our Father is a Spirit with heavenly DNA, and His new-creation children are spiritual beings also. Scripture furthermore tells us that our heavenly Father is the Father of spiritual children, being called the *"Father of spirits"* (Heb. 12:9). When a person is born again, the capacity to touch God in the spiritual realm is restored.

The Christian, then, finds himself in a dilemma between the flesh and the spirit. When a person is saved, their spirit has been made alive but the carnal nature wars against the spirit within them. Both the flesh and the spirit vie for control.

Have you ever tried to mix oil and water? They are both liquids, but they are very different substances. Molecules of oil are attracted to each other but are repelled by water molecules. In the same way, flesh and spirit repel one another. Oil doesn't intermingle with water and flesh doesn't connect with spirit. Paul says, *"For the flesh lusts against the Spirit, and the Spirit against the flesh; and these are contrary to another, so that you do not do the things that you wish"* (Gal. 5:17).

## CALMING OUR SOUL

To commune with God spirit-to-Spirit, Christians must learn how to deal with the flesh and connect in the spirit. The fallen nature of man is not at all like God's nature. They don't mix. Either flesh rules or spirit rules at any given time—they can't be intermingled and both rule at the same time.

We must learn, then, to actively participate in maintaining this spiritual connection with the Lord. Quieting the flesh and yielding to the Spirit of God accomplishes this. The psalmist wrote, *"Surely I have calmed and quieted my soul, like a weaned child with his mother"* (Ps. 131:2). And Paul reminds us: *"If we live in the Spirit, let us also walk in the Spirit"* (Gal. 5:25).

God has given us tools to use throughout our life in order to better connect with Him and walk in wholeness. We can only give what we have received. Most believers have not known the easy way to deal with the issues of life and have simply coped with fears, pain, and shame. If we are still wounded in a particular area, we do not have an anointing to minister healing to someone else in that area.

Hurt people hurt people. When we are hurting, we will identify with the same hurts in others (trigger one another's wounds) or project our own issues on others. Hurt people overreact to even mild stimulation, lash out at others, withdraw from relationships, put up walls, see life through distorted lenses, and can be easily offended.

But healed people heal people. After the Lord brings healing to us, an anointing flows through the scar to bring healing to others. When we are healed, even the area where we were wounded the most can become our greatest anointing to minister life to the hurting. C. J. Mahaney wrote, "Because we are the most forgiven people in the world, we should be the most forgiving people in the world."[1] And that is what this book is all about.

## NOTE

1.   C. J. Mahaney, *Pastoral Leadership for Manhood and Womanhood,* ed. Wayne Grudem and Dennis Rainey, (Wheaton, Ill.: Crossway, 2002), 202.

Chapter 1

# Touching God

## Disillusioned to Despair

How long have you been frustrated, trying to get help, wanting relief from pain, or seeking more of God? How is your level of hope? Maybe a little on the low side? Are you weary, longing for the elusive "more" of God, but secretly wondering if this is all you'll ever have of God experiences? Yet deep down in your heart of hearts, a faintly glowing ember still burns.

"But," you might say, "many have promised so much yet delivered so little." You may be secretly tired of church life as you know it: conferences, books, and retreats put you to sleep. The problem is that God created you for Himself, for communion with Him. And anything short of that leaves you with an emptiness that is never filled.

If what you have tried so far hasn't satisfied the longing of your soul, then maybe you should try another way. Even as you read this, however, discouragement will whisper in your ear, "I already know that. I read the books, took the courses, went to hear anointed preachers. So what next?"

## SPIRITUAL DROPOUT

Forty-six percent of genuinely born-again Christians no longer bother to attend a local church, which is so valuable for growth in the Christian life. Most of these believers, who really love Jesus with all their hearts, feel stuck in their spiritual experience with God. They are struggling with offenses or rejection, they have become discouraged in their search for answers, and they don't know how to make Christianity work for them in a practical way.

Many feel like they are dying of spiritual thirst, but church has seemed like a dry well, so they finally give up on going. Some of them were wounded by church leadership, causing them to feel angry and disillusioned; some feel betrayed because they got involved in a church that was overly controlling. A vast number of Christians were wounded by other church members and have never been able to get over it. And still others have fallen into sin and have disqualified themselves because of shame and condemnation.

Church life has promised much but failed to deliver for them. How many more are still in the church but are living in quiet despair? We're not saying that these are valid reasons to not attend a local church (every Christian should be involved in one), but they are valid areas of pain that cause us to be disillusioned and quit.

Their experiences are far from the abundant life Jesus promised (see John 10:10), and they are far from what the normal Christian life looks like throughout the Book of Acts. The stories of the saints of old tantalize us with the possibility of glorious intimacy with God. There is so much more than what we're currently experiencing.

Christians shouldn't be living like spiritual paupers when we have been promised the banqueting table of the riches of God and the communion found in His chambers. This is the deepest longing of all our hearts—the very reason we were created.

What if we told you that you are about to learn the secrets of those who discovered the reality of God and the treasures of the Spirit? What if we told you how to make real-life Christianity work? There are hidden truths just waiting to be discovered. There are some simple keys that make it all work.

## The Bliss of Touching God

Communion with God is the unspeakably glorious experience for which Christ died—the goal of the cross. Christ was crucified and resurrected to open the way for us to *experience* God—His heart, His mind, and His will—not just *know* about Him.

When Christ died on the cross, the veil of the temple was torn from top to bottom, enabling every person on earth to enter God's manifest presence. This realm of unspeakable love, joy, and peace is where we are now invited to live moment by moment, day by day. The cross enables us to experience *constant communion* with God and feel the bliss of touching Love Himself.

Does this sound too good to be true? We can assure you that it isn't. Christ suffered to redeem our lives from darkness and usher us into the glory of His tangible presence. So why would we settle for anything less?

For centuries believers from all nations and denominations have sought this magnificent communion with God. Their goal has been simple but radical: the experience of *union*, the sublime joy of uninterrupted relationship, and the ever-deepening oneness with the Beloved.

We may have read of this experience of union with God by saints of old. We may even have heard recent testimonies from pulpits and platforms. But most of us, although we may believe such experiences are true, retreat to our prayer closets and inwardly groan: *How, Lord? When? Where might I find this experience with the lover of my soul?*

We groan because we know that such union is possible and paid for by the blood shed at Calvary. We know we were born to experience God. Indeed, the deepest desire of every heart is to experience His presence—not just occasionally, but moment by moment. Nothing will ever satisfy this deepest need but the experience of His constant presence with us, every moment of every day.

We seek His tangible company as one friend cherishes the company of another. We yearn for His touch as a child longs to be held. We earnestly desire His embrace even as a bride desires her husband. We crave for Him—we desire Him more than our necessary food.

The Father desires that His sons and daughters learn how to live like the biblical patriarch Enoch, who *"walked with God"* (Gen. 5:24), and like Adam and Eve, who walked with the Lord *"in the cool of the day"* (Gen. 3:8). But the cross has given us an even greater intimacy with God than Enoch, Adam, or Eve ever had. The Holy Spirit now resides within each and every believer. We all can now experience oneness with Christ even as Christ experiences oneness with the Father (see John 17:11). We can experience abiding in Christ 24/7.

## CONTINUAL COMMUNION WITH GOD

Now is the time for all Christians to learn this most glorious lesson of the overcomer's life: how to walk in continual communion with God. We are being called to come into *"the measure of the stature of the fullness of Christ"* (Eph. 4:13), to become the sons and daughters of God who truly represent Christ in the world.

But how does this happen? It comes through understanding how to touch His presence, feel His feelings, think His thoughts, and do His will—not our own. We invite you to journey with us into this experiential union with Christ. Most of us believe that this is possible—at least theoretically and doctrinally—but few have actually experienced this intimacy, even momentarily, and even fewer are practicing God's presence all day, every day.

But this lesson of communing with Christ is extremely simple to learn. In fact, any child is capable of experiencing this most basic grace of the Christian life. God has already made Himself fully and readily available to the young and the old, the foolish and the learned, the broken, the poor, the desperate, and the lonely (see 1 Cor. 1:26-31).

For many years we have been teaching believers how to abide in Christ and thousands of lives have been transformed in the process. The Lord has healed marriages, physical sicknesses, broken hearts, and panic attacks, and He has become the ever-present Prince of Peace for many, replacing toxic emotions with Himself.

As we learn to touch God's heart, our emotions will be transformed. And as His divine emotions become ours, the joy of His heart radiating from our lives will draw the lost and broken to the light of His glory within the children of

God. His presence radiating from within us will bring transformation to nations and revival to the earth.

## ONE WORD

Communion with Christ is simple and fast, and is summed up in one word. But before we tell you what that word is, we must warn you! It is a word that offends many Christians, as though we are suggesting they have failed to be a model Christian. You may think you know what it means; you may even believe you know all there is to know about it. You may even say, "I've already tried that." But set all that aside for just a moment.

Picture this: Imagine that you think you have a nice "crystal" paperweight. It is beautiful, but it just sits unused on your desk. What if you suddenly discovered that it was really a flawless diamond worth billions of dollars?[1] That could change everything in your life.

So how does communion with Christ happen? What is the one word that can change everything and sums up our walk with God? It is simply this: forgiveness. Communion with Christ happens through the most heavenly lifestyle you can imagine—a lifestyle of forgiveness. Through learning how to practice forgiveness throughout the day, individuals, families, and churches have truly been "born again, again" by experiencing uninterrupted intimacy with God.

Forgiveness has the potential to change *everything* in your life. It is not just for salvation, major betrayals and wounds, or for the confessional. It is the God-tool for maintaining a 24/7-heart connection with Christ. But if it is so powerful and simple, why do so few experience this level of fellowship with God?

## BLOCKED BY OFFENSES

Our experience of God's tangible Spirit is blocked or interrupted by our offenses and sins. To experience Christ without ceasing, we must receive and release forgiveness continually.

Most Christians, however, do not know how to forgive. We may say we forgive someone who has offended us—but forgiveness is not just saying the right words. We may pray fervently with tears—but forgiveness is not just an emotional release. We may even determine to forgive by making a quality decision—but forgiveness is not an act of exerting our own will. Forgiveness is much more than mere mental assent, feeling sorry for oneself, or doing a good deed. It is a supernatural encounter with Christ the forgiver.

This is the secret of communion with God. As we learn to experience supernatural forgiveness—releasing Christ the forgiver from our innermost being—we learn to live in the presence of God. But many times there are constant setbacks in our life, offenses that keep us from abiding in Christ.

## CONSTANT SETBACKS

Kevin, a 26-year-old Iraq war veteran, was tormented by flashbacks and recurrent nightmares. While on patrol in

Iraq, Kevin's Humvee[2] hit an IED.[3] The Humvee was blown apart, tearing off Kevin's leg at mid-thigh. His best friend lay dying, his face virtually gone. Debilitating fear and survivor's guilt haunted Kevin from that time on.

After Kevin returned home to the states, he could hardly keep a job. He was diagnosed with Post Traumatic Stress Injury (PTSI). Irritability, angry rages, nightmares, and suicidal thoughts continually plagued him. His marriage was in shambles. But Kevin learned to yield to Christ the forgiver and was completely healed and delivered in one prayer session. He had his life back. What had been life-destroying trauma turned to true freedom.

Few of us have experienced the trauma of war, but how often during the day do we feel stressed or offended? If you're like most people, you probably live with intermittent if not constant anxiety, worry, or annoyance. Minor offenses and emotional setbacks—with your spouse, children, coworkers, or strangers—are ongoing struggles.

Many of us go to bed with a few regrets and wake up with worries. We're angered by slow drivers and frustrated in long grocery lines. We feel emotionally spent after long hours at work or months without work. Or we're brokenhearted from a painful marriage or a wayward child. We've grown slightly weary as we age. We can't stop overeating, overspending, watching TV, surfing the Internet, yelling at our spouse, or criticizing ourselves. At our most desperate moments, we may even dip into carnality with a few too many beers or a violent movie.

We think we've dealt with our inner demons, wounds, and offenses, but continue to feel hurt or frustrated by family, coworkers, and friends. And if we're truly honest with ourselves, we oftentimes feel hurt by or frustrated with God.

When we're anxious and stressed, afraid or depressed, it means that God is not in the equation. It's not that God isn't present, but we're not experiencing His tangible presence because we are walking in unforgiveness.

Everyone can learn how to deal with unhealthy emotions and habits, and begin to commune with Christ in a truly life-giving way. We don't need willpower, fasting, diets, ministers, or even a miracle to take place. We only need to learn this simple way of prayer to yield to Christ the forgiver whenever we feel an offense arise. And as quick as we do that, peace with Christ is restored, as well as an awareness of His presence.

## GOD-TOOLS

Years ago, I (Dennis) was in our front yard trimming an overgrown bush with manual clippers when a neighbor noticed me struggling. The neighbor took pity on me and walked over with the right tool—a powerful electric trimmer. "Here, try this instead," he said, laughing. "You've been doing it the hard way!" Needless to say, the rest of my work was much easier.

We have been trying to do Christianity the hard way. But the good news is that God has given us efficient, powerful "God-tools" for dismantling painful, ungodly emotions and thoughts. Let's consider this Scripture from Second Corinthians 10:4-5 in The Message Bible:

> We use our powerful God-tools for smashing warped philosophies, tearing down barriers erected against the truth of God, fitting every loose thought and emotion and impulse into the structure of life shaped by Christ.

Jesus has given us powerful God-tools that will take care of all of our issues. He has given us the tools necessary to bring our wayward thoughts, willful impulses, and unpleasant emotions under the control of the Holy Spirit. The purpose of touching God is to equip us to use the tools we've been given.

The most powerful God-tool in our spiritual arsenal is the tool of supernatural forgiveness. This one key, if properly applied, can solve the majority of our problems. But the answer only works when it is a genuine supernatural transaction. Christ the forgiver can and will replace every toxic emotion with His peace that transcends understanding. As we learn this simple way of prayer, we begin to learn to abide in Christ.

## A Supernatural Exchange

Debbie lived a life of unimaginable emotional pain because of her past. As a child, she was regularly beaten; as a teen, she was sexually molested; and as an adult, she was raped. She'd had three abortions. Finally, she saw her son murdered—and watched the killer walk free.

Debbie was so traumatized by her history that she had trouble functioning in daily life. She wanted to forgive those who abused her, but just didn't know how. We prayed with Debbie, and in less than 20 minutes of prayer she was emotionally healed by the greatest force in the universe. Her sorrow turned to lasting peace. She learned how to present her deepest wounds to Christ and experienced the freedom of forgiveness. And Debbie excitedly told us that she intended to use what she had learned to help others.

Even though she knew it was the right thing to do, Debbie couldn't forgive her abusers on her own. Why not? Because only Christ the forgiver can truly forgive. Debbie was emotionally healed from her traumatic past because she experienced God forgiving her enemies. That's what God does, and that's who God is.

Forgiveness is a supernatural, divine exchange: Christ in exchange for our pain. Debbie learned how to yield to Christ within and let Him do all the work. Now instead of grief, Debbie yields to God and experiences peace in everyday life by practicing forgiveness.

Few have suffered like Debbie, but we all face pain, fears, and difficulties in life, from the death of loved ones to the daily stress at work, home, or school. Our troubles may be relatively minor, but we all encounter stress that impacts our life in negative ways. And because of this, we have all been taught what forgiveness is. But each of us come to the table with our own preconceived ideas of what forgiveness really means and how it is to be applied to our life.

## TEACHING FORGIVENESS

Experiencing Christ the forgiver like this can be taught and learned. For decades, we've helped thousands of average Christians from many denominations and backgrounds learn how to let Christ the forgiver take their emotional pain and replace it with Himself.

We've taught these simple 1-2-3 steps of forgiveness to new believers and seasoned saints, to Protestants and Catholics, Episcopalians and Baptists, charismatics and evangelicals. We've taught them to pastors, priests, and nuns, CEOs and PhDs, the poor and millionaires, teens and preschoolers, as well as truck drivers and missionaries. No pain is too great and no person too damaged or addicted.

If you follow these simple steps, you will learn Christ's way of supernatural forgiveness and overcome hurts, fears, loneliness, anger, guilt, shame, and other toxic pathways in your mind and body—quickly and permanently. As you learn to yield to the tangible presence of Christ, He will displace every painful emotion with His peace.

Communion with God is available to you, no matter what your emotional pain and life traumas have been. This is the unspeakably wonderful promise for which Christ died, the joy He wants us to know: *"looking unto Jesus, the author and finisher of our faith, who for the joy that was set before Him endured the cross, despising the shame, and has sat down at the right hand of the throne of God"* (Heb. 12:2).

## NOTES

1. The largest polished diamond in the world is the Golden Jubilee Diamond, which is 545.6 carats and is valued between $4–$12 million.

2. The military name for these are HMMWV, which stands for High Mobility Multi-Purpose Wheeled Vehicle.

3. Improvised Explosive Device.

Chapter 2

# OUR STORIES

## BORN AGAIN

About four months after I (Dennis) was born again, I was minding my own business when I had a vision. I had an impression of the Godhead: the Father, Son, and the Holy Spirit. I also had a sense I was being indwelt and infused with tremendous power. Then, with my eyes wide open, in the air right in front of me were suspended letters of living life: GRAND BOOK AND BIBLE. Even though I read them like I would read anything else, it was as if my entire being was absorbed into them.

Grand Book and Bible was a Christian bookstore about a mile from my house. When I got there, I was grabbed by the arm of one of the women working, and she said, "There is a man in this store that you must meet." She took me over to meet the author of the only Christian book I had read in the period since being saved (besides the Bible).

I introduced myself, we talked for a bit, and then he said to me, "You need to go to the Christian businessmen's luncheon." So I went to the luncheon and received the baptism in the Holy Spirit, and I began to speak in a supernatural language that day.

From that moment on, there has always been a constant awareness of God's presence in my life. There has never been a moment that I wasn't aware of carrying precious cargo. I liken it to a woman who is pregnant. She has to go about her business, but she's always aware that she is carrying something precious, something she must feed, nurture, and protect even as she goes about her daily routine. And the feeling of carrying His presence and peace with me constantly has never left.

## PRACTICING THE PRESENCE

So as a new believer, I spent hours simply enjoying the presence of God in prayer. I longed to experience that same peace throughout the whole day—to experience Christ moment by moment. And God met that desire and taught me how to abide in Him.

It has now been more than 30 years since the Lord taught me how to unceasingly commune with Christ through these simple steps of supernatural forgiveness. I have since lived most of my days in uninterrupted peace. I'm able to touch the presence of God easily, abiding in Christ whether I'm working, driving, eating, or resting. And if I ever lose this peace momentarily, I know how to get it back quickly.

The writings of a seventeenth-century monk, Brother Lawrence, inspired my spiritual journey. Brother Lawrence provided an example of how to live every moment in unceasing adoration of God. He called this way of life "the practice of the presence of God." With every dish Brother Lawrence washed and every floor he scrubbed, he sought to love God and experience His presence.

Much like Brother Lawrence, I learned that prayer was not something that I did, but was Someone with whom I lived in constant contact with, no matter the activity. I learned that I could commune with God while doing the dishes, napping, or going about my work. He was with me in all that I was doing, so why couldn't I be conscious of Him?

As I became acclimated to the love nature of God as a young Christian, I began to develop a keen sensitivity to other people. When they were nervous, angry, or hurting, I could sense their emotions in my spirit. Despite my growing discernment, however, I still had plenty of hurts, wounds, and rejections of my own to battle. God was about to heal me.

## Emotional Healing

A pivotal moment came the year following my conversion. A spirit that had harassed me for my entire life was completely broken off. (This was in 1976.) I had been asked to offer my testimony at a small meeting, and was excited about sharing all the Lord had done for me. I was invited because of the richness of my testimony and the vision I had before about the bookstore. So I went up to the platform, looked out over the audience of about 40 people, and I just froze. Fear and shame so gripped me that I just walked right off the platform.

I loved Jesus with all my heart, desired to serve God, and had rich experiences in prayer. I had no idea of what was going on as I was on the platform. So I went home and cried out to God, "God, I've been called to preach. I've been having all of these wonderful experiences. So what is wrong with me?" As I cried out to the Lord in prayer, I immediately saw myself as a young 9-year-old boy with clenched fists, hating myself because I couldn't control my body. It suddenly all came rushing back to me in that moment.

You see, I had been a bed-wetter for many years as a child. I now felt the same shame and hatred toward myself that I had felt as a child decades before. As an adult, I now knew that it was a sin to hate *other* people, but the Lord showed me that it was also wrong for me to hate myself. I said, "God, I knew it was wrong to hold unforgiveness toward other people, but even toward myself too?"

I yielded and allowed Christ the forgiver to flow to and through my pain. I instantly experienced the Lord touching my heart as He replaced my shame and anger with His supernatural peace. I was flooded with a sense of God's presence once again. At the same time, the spirit, which felt like a slimy, burglar's stocking mask, began to lift off of me.

The next day I went to my local church and the first thing my pastor said was, "Dennis, I want you to share your testimony." So I walked up to the pulpit and said, "I don't know if everyone's going to understand this, but I like me." And they all laughed and thought, *Wow, this guy has some issues here.* But I was so full of the joy of the Lord because for the first time I received myself the way God received me. I was free. I was forgiven. I had forgiven myself and the hatred and shame were completely gone. It was total freedom. The shame that had been blocking my practicing of God's presence was gone!

## TEACH ME TO PRAY

I had a good prayer life during this time, spending hours in God's presence. And one day, as I was praying, God said to me, "Ask Me to teach you how to pray." At first I was a little stunned because I thought what I had been doing was quite sufficient—everything I learned I learned in prayer. But He told me to ask Him to teach me how to pray, so I humbled myself and said, "Sure, teach me how to pray." To my surprise, it immediately began that day—one thought coming from the heart of God, bombarding me continuously.

The thought was this: "Dennis, I'm giving you My undivided attention." Every single day for about a month God never changed the subject. I simply received it and soaked in it. I let it wash over me, absorbed it, and I became a partaker of what God was speaking to me.

It was only in hindsight that I understood that the shame and rejection was continually being washed out of me over that period of time. But while it was happening, it did something else quite entirely. I had never known such acceptance, such affection, and such love before in my life. And these were not just concepts that I received, but they were impressions that I owned and absorbed—totally new feelings I had never had.

Nobody came up to me and said, "Dennis, you're my constant delight and I'm giving you my undivided attention." But rather, all of a sudden, by the end of the four weeks of being bombarded with so much affection, attention, and acceptance, I wanted to burst on the inside. So I finally cried out, "God, I want to reciprocate. I've got to! I can't do it like You, God. I can't think of You every minute of every day; I'll try, but I can't do it. But I do want to reciprocate."

And then that's when I heard God say to me, "You can. I've given you the equipment."

So I learned that *any* toxic emotion *interrupts* practicing the presence of God, but as soon as I yielded to Christ the forgiver whenever I encountered an unpleasant situation, a hurtful person, or when I needed forgiveness, I returned to communing with God. God *always* showed up to heal me—without fail. Jesus is true to His Word: He *will* deliver us from every one of our pains and sorrows.

## MEETING JENNIFER

In 1997, I had a meeting where I ministered to a Christian woman that was a really difficult case. This lady basically had a meltdown in front of everyone present. It was like she had everything in the book and felt like everything was wrong with her. She even began writhing on the floor. So I simply said, "We're not going to make a big scene here." I knelt down beside her and ministered emotional healing. I dealt with some of her mental strongholds, brought them down, and did some deliverance with her. It lasted only about ten minutes. She stood up after that time, her countenance changed, a smile on her face, and everyone was talking about how fast it went.

There was another woman who had come to attend the meetings. She was smart—she was a psychologist, a counselor, and a ThD. She watched me as I ministered to that woman and saw the freedom that came to her so quickly. She later said to me, "When you're done, I want you to pray for me and I want to pray for you." And that was the phrase God had given me earlier: "You're going to know your wife because she's going to pray for you and ask you to pray for her."

## JENNIFER'S STORY

The weekend that we met for the first time, I (Jennifer) saw Dennis pray with an extremely distraught woman at a Christian conference. The woman, Amanda, had an emotional meltdown and collapsed on the floor weeping. Everyone froze in their tracks. I was watching this take place and then thought to myself, *Five or ten years of counseling might help such a broken soul.* But this was before I met Dennis and learned these simple steps of forgiveness.

Dennis knelt beside Amanda, who had become hysterical. He began to coach her step by step, walking her through this simple process of supernatural forgiveness. Christ the forgiver quickly and easily dealt with her emotional pain. In less than ten minutes, Amanda was up on her feet, smiling and calm, testifying that her emotional pain was gone.

Astounded, I understood that the rapid healing steps she witnessed could bring emotional healing to a world full of hurting people—including the most "mature" Christians still carrying wounds from childhood or battling daily stress at work, in ministry, around the family dinner table, or at school. I realized that whatever Dennis had done was a much faster and more thorough approach than anything I had ever witnessed before.

As a Christian counselor, I had been very discouraged by the slow progress of my hurting clients. After months, and sometimes even years, of prayer and counseling, many sincere Christians continued to suffer from negative emotions. No matter what was tried—classic or innovative therapies, healing and deliverance prayers, and Bible instruction— most couldn't experience God's peace and joy consistently and permanently. Some found relief for the short term, but long-term emotional healing was very slow in coming. Even Christians who had been believers for 20 or 30 years continued to suffer from the wounds of the past. I was bewildered.

Many other Christians in the healing professions confirmed my experience. A medical doctor who worked with Christians struggling with addictions once told me, "I know the Bible says believers are supposed to be new creations in Christ, but I just see the same old issues." Experiencing similar failures, another counselor had come to believe that people had to be fairly well-adjusted at salvation or they would be too wounded to ever be "used much" in Christian ministry.

I myself was a wounded Christian. Having suffered the death of my first husband from lymphoma, I struggled to raise my two children on my own, still carrying emotional wounds from my own childhood and difficult marriage. Fortunately, God brought Dennis to me as not only my new husband, but also as my teacher and mentor in the ways of supernatural forgiveness.

As soon as we married, I asked Dennis to teach me. We began to pray intentional prayers of forgiveness together regularly, almost daily. I was not content to pray through just the major issues in my life, but wanted to "go for broke." After two months, I found myself marvelously transformed. I could hardly remember what I had been like before. Fear was gone. My emotional pain had been washed away completely. Work was no longer stressful. Life was a delight. Now I knew what the joy of the Lord really felt like. Instead of being demanding and controlling, I became emotionally available and trusting. I also experienced ongoing peace instead of sorrow and anxiety.

I discovered a deep yearning to teach these secrets of healing and peace to hurting Christians. I had found the God-tool that not only healed my own hidden fears, anger, and shame, but also those of others. I was truly on a journey with God.

## TRANSFORMED OUR MARRIAGE

This understanding of communion with God and walking in a lifestyle of forgiveness actually began with Dennis and I in our personal prayer time. Our prayer times together were usually pretty quiet—we both liked to enjoy His presence. And as we were having a soaking prayer time, we had very yielded hearts, and suddenly His presence came rushing into the room. We knew it was God Himself coming into that room and invading our space.

And when He came in, we both blurted out two Scriptures simultaneously. Dennis said, "This is when two or three are gathered in My name," making a reference to Matthew 18:20; and I burst out, "This is one accord," referencing Acts 2:1. We felt that in His presence we were being supernaturally knit together. We were, of course, already knit together through the marriage covenant, and we felt like we already had a prophetic marriage. We already knew God put the two of us together for His kingdom purposes, not just for us to enjoy one another. But this was supernaturally above and beyond even what God had already done with us. It was an expression of anointing of His peace that was tied directly to unity.

So there was a bond of peace that was created that day, a deeper bonding than what we had previously experienced. We were shocked at this encounter in our prayer time, but we were also eager to find out what it would look like as we ministered together.

Our very first meeting after that took place was in Greer, South Carolina. While teaching at the meeting, the weight and heaviness of peace came down and rested in the room. Some people were sitting, others were standing in the altar area, worshiping with their eyes closed. And Dennis sat on the platform and was led by the Spirit to point to about seven different people who were standing in the audience—some of them saw him point at them while others did not. But as soon as Dennis pointed to them, they fell to the floor under the weight of God's peace.

And when they got up, their testimonies were almost identical. They said, "We feel a supernatural knitting to our pastor and to the leadership in this place." It was like a mini knitting together by the Spirit of God. It was a kind of unity we had not seen before—it was not fabricated or conjured up. It was truly supernatural.

God had taught us both to walk in supernatural peace, uninterrupted fellowship with Him, and a unity of marriage we had never experienced before. He was beginning to use us to bring others into this experience as well.

Chapter 3

# THE POWER OF
# TESTIMONIES

## EMOTIONAL HEALING MYTHS

Emotions and prayers for emotional healing have gotten a bad rap in some schools of thought. However, our emotions are important to God. Do you remember that He created us in His image, with a mind, will, and emotions? So when God wants to restore us to His image through what Jesus has done for us on the cross, then He wants to restore our emotional well-being. He is not interested in the "spiritual" side of our lives; He is interested in our lives.

As we experience life throughout the years, the truth is that our heart gets broken—not like a broken bone per se, but wounds and offenses block aspects of our heart, cutting us off from feeling certain emotions or connecting with God. But God is near to us during those times. Psalm 34:18 tells us that *"the Lord is near to those who have a broken heart, and saves such as have a contrite spirit."* And Jesus Himself announced that to *"heal the brokenhearted"* was included in His job description (see Luke 4:16-20).

God is after our heart and longs to see us restored and healed in every area—spirit, soul, and body. But many of us have bought into myths about emotional healing that we need to sort out. We're going to give you a list of emotional healing myths and their corresponding truths. It is important to spend some time praying over the corresponding truth if you have bought into the myth.

**Myth:** The past is all taken care of at the time of conversion—everything is "under the blood."

**Truth:** Yes, legally Jesus paid the price for full freedom, healing, and deliverance. But each believer must receive and appropriate their inheritance for it to be effective in their life.

**Myth:** You don't have to "dig up the past."

**Truth:** You shouldn't analyze yourself, but allow God to search your heart.

**Myth:** "Just get over it!"

**Truth:** If we could fix ourselves by pretending everything is okay, then we wouldn't need Jesus to be our Comforter.

**Myth:** When God heals, He *erases* the memory.

**Truth:** When God heals, He leaves the memory intact, but heals the pain. It becomes part of our testimony and also carries an anointing to minister healing to others.

**Myth:** If you *understand* why someone did something, you can let it go.

**Truth:** Understanding alone does not bring healing. The adult mind may rationalize, but that doesn't bring healing for the emotions. God heals whatever part of the heart we present to Him, but He cannot heal an excuse.

God wants to break into our world and heal us of the emotional pain and trauma we have been carrying with us for years. But He can only do it if we allow Christ to work in us and through us. And if we're buying into the myths of emotional healing, then we're going to have a hard time surrendering to Christ, allowing Him to rule in every area of our life. Meditating on these truths should demolish many of the strongholds we've been taught over the years as it relates to emotional healing.

## THE POWER OF TESTIMONIES AND THE FAITHFULNESS OF GOD

Why is it so powerful when a Christian shares their salvation testimony? A personal testimony always carries an anointing because it bears witness to a supernatural God encounter. When God touches a life, He always leaves a deposit of His divine nature on it. Salvation is just the beginning though—it is only our *first* testimony.

In addition to salvation, believers testify about miracles of all kinds, answered prayers, physical healings, emotional healings, divine appointments, and financial blessings. Testimonies are just us telling again what God has done for us in our lives. And when we tell our testimony of what God has done for us, it creates a supernatural expectation for God to do it again in the people who hear it.

It is important for us to keep a journal or a record of what God has done in our life. That way we can constantly remember how He has acted for us, and we will always have an account to tell others in times of need. All of us seem to have short memories of the good things the Lord does for us. We too easily forget God's faithfulness.

In the Bible, we read the story of the children of Israel, who were miraculously led out of Egypt and witnessed the parting of the Red Sea, only to despair three days later when the water was bitter at Marah.

> *So Moses brought Israel from the Red Sea; then they went out into the Wilderness of Shur. And they went three days in the wilderness and found no water. Now when they came to Marah, they could not drink the waters of Marah, for they were bitter. Therefore the name of it was called Marah.*

> *And the people complained against Moses, saying,*
> *"What shall we drink?" So he cried out to the*
> *Lord, and the Lord showed him a tree. When he*
> *cast it into the waters, the waters were made sweet*
> (Exodus 15:22-25).

Even though God just showed Himself mighty on their behalf, they still soon forgot the works of the Lord and everything He had done for them. Keeping a record of what God does on our behalf helps us not to forget God's works. In times of abundance and times of need it is important to keep a record of His faithfulness.

God revealed His intention toward us through Jeremiah:

> *I will bless you with a future filled with hope—a*
> *future of success, not of suffering. You will turn*
> *back to Me and ask for help, and I will answer your*
> *prayers. You will worship Me with all your heart,*
> *and I will be with you* (Jeremiah 29:11-13 CEV).

It is of utmost importance to remember how God has cared for us. We should look at our past to see how God has moved on our behalf and how He has been faithful to us. Then, once our past deliverances are in sight, we can begin to look at our present circumstances, calling to mind what the future holds for us. God has a plan and a future for us.

## Marriages Supernaturally United

God's peace and presence affects marriages in a supernatural way. For a lack of a better term, we called the experience Jennifer and I had "one accord." After that experience, there were so many people who came up to us at our meetings and said, "You two have a oneness anointing." And we had no idea what to do with that.

But after we had our experience in prayer, where we both blurted out Scriptures, the next meeting we did at a church we had multitudes of married couples come up to us and ask us to pray for them during a fellowship time. We didn't ask for it to happen nor were we expecting it. It was then that we learned that God was doing something with the oneness anointing, a peace deepening relationships.

We prayed for them when they came up and taught them to melt together and experience each other spirit-to-spirit. We were surprised how many husbands and wives love each other and communicate with each other, but they don't commune with one another. They talk about life, about the kids, and about finances, but they don't intimately commune with one another; they don't know each other by the spirit. There is actually an opportunity to melt into each other and know one another by the spirit.

That meeting was the beginning of couples' coming to us for prayer and to experience supernatural oneness in their marriages. We later incorporated this understanding into our marriage seminar. One out of 20 couples actually felt like they had a good spirit-to-spirit connection. We basically helped them into a place of learning Christ the forgiver on the inside, breaking down any walls of hostility between the two, and then had them come forward so we could pray for them. God began to bring many couples into "one accord," allowing healing and forgiveness to flow.

## PHYSICAL HEALINGS

Through forgiveness prayers, we have since seen the Lord heal and deliver many thousands from emotional traumas, mild to severe, often with accompanying physical healings. It's as if when we get the soul right, God begins to bring healing to the entire body. People have come to us who have terminal illnesses, and the worst part of the sickness sometimes is the torment that comes with it. These people were believers and had mental torment about their sicknesses. So we would tell them we wanted to bring peace to them first on the inside, then let Christ the healer rise up and manifest Himself in their bodies.

One of the most amazing things is that we rarely pray for healing when the peace of God shows up. We simply pray for them to come into that supernatural exchange of peace and deal with the toxic emotions, and healing has almost always been the by-product. Out of all the supernatural healings we've seen, we almost never directly ask for them, except perhaps on rare occasions. We can only remember one occasion where we directly went for the physical healing.

A young man experienced emotional healing and was subsequently healed of color blindness. There was also a woman who had arthritis in her hands so bad that she was in the hospital. She was bitter at her mother for some past trauma. We told her that Christ would manifest as the forgiver if she would allow Him to forgive through her. As she listened and released forgiveness toward her mother, the arthritis, right before our very eyes, straightened out and disappeared completely. We were not praying for arthritis to be healed in any way. She was simply forgiving her mother and the supernatural took place in her body.

## TESTIMONIES OF FORGIVENESS PRAYERS

Here are just a few of the testimonies of the emotional trauma we've seen healed from praying forgiveness prayers. Many believers have testified that this simple God-tool of forgiveness has had profound emotional and physical benefits.

Delivered from chronic shame: "I carried shame for my entire life. I didn't realize how it colored my world. After learning how to release Christ the forgiver, I can look people in the eye now. I feel freer, cleaner, and more emotionally whole than ever before."

Delivered from chronic anger: "I asked God to root out the cause of my ongoing anger. Immediately, the Holy Spirit showed me scenes of rejection and ridicule by friends and teachers. As each person came to my mind, I released Christ the forgiver to them. The scenes unfolded in a reverse chronological order, and finally the Holy Spirit led me to the memory of being a bed wetter. My parents made me wear diapers until I was 10, and I endured years of shame and humiliation because of it. I released Christ the forgiver to myself and my parents. The anger and rejection were replaced with peace—and I'm now filled with incredible joy!"

Delivered from chronic rejection: "I was completely delivered and healed from a spirit of rejection that plagued me my whole life. Through the lifestyle of forgiveness, I was set free. I now feel *a part* of life and not on the outside looking in. Forgiveness is amazing!"

Delivered from torment and mere head knowledge: "I used to experience much oppression and torment, and lived my Christian life in my head. As a result of these simple lessons, I have learned to walk in the Spirit and experience ongoing peace and communion with the Lord. My life has been transformed."

Delivered from deep-rooted bitterness: "I thought I had totally forgiven everyone in my life, but I hadn't. I felt a wall in my gut when certain people came to mind. I had only mentally forgiven them. My emotions were toxic and unchanged. As I learned to yield every pain to Christ within, His peace flowed to my bitterness—and now I live from that peace. This was so liberating that I eagerly do the same with everyone, including myself, whenever anything disrupts my peace."

Delivered from sexual abuse: "I was severely abused as a child by my father and brother, and have struggled for years to forgive, trust, and love again. After I released Christ the forgiver to my abusers, heaven's peace came upon me. The Lord told me to look in Ezekiel 36:26: *'I will give you a new heart and put a new spirit within you.'* My new heart feels wonderful!"

Delivered from marital conflicts: "As newlyweds, we couldn't stop fighting and triggering each others' wounds— but we started to see results the first night we started praying forgiveness prayers. We have grown so much emotionally through this forgiveness lifestyle. With these simple tools, we were not only able to establish a firm foundation for our marriage, but we are also learning to tap into our oneness anointing. Our marriage is truly transformed!"

Christ the forgiver can indeed accomplish a year's worth of therapy in 30 or 40 minutes of prayer. The first step to freedom—for ourselves and for our loved ones—is in grasping that forgiveness is not a mere doctrine, but a Person named Jesus Christ.

Chapter 4

# God-Tools

*We use our powerful God-tools for...fitting
every loose thought and emotion and
impulse into the structure of life shaped by
Christ* (2 Corinthians 10:4-5 MSG).

## Forgiveness Is a Person

Among the last words of Jesus on the cross are the most
powerful words ever uttered: *"Father, forgive them, for they
do not know what they do"* (Luke 23:34). And Father God
did just that—forgave the entire world of every sin ever committed. Jesus died and was raised again to usher in God's
unspeakable mercy and forgiveness for all humankind.

The next action Jesus took was to forgive one of the criminals hanging beside Him on the cross. The criminal said, *"Lord, remember me when You come into Your kingdom"* (Luke 23:42). And Jesus immediately responded, *"Assuredly, I say to you, today you will be with Me in Paradise"* (Luke 23:43). The moment the thief asked Jesus to remember him, Jesus immediately responded that he would be with Him in Paradise that day—the thief instantly received forgiveness the moment he asked for it. He was redeemed.

We may believe the biblical truth of forgiveness in principle, but if we struggle with *any* measure of toxic emotions or stress, from minor worries to deep-seated bitterness, we have not learned how to forgive others, nor have we truly learned how to receive forgiveness from God for ourselves.

Forgiveness is not just saying the words, "I forgive them, Lord," or "Forgive me, Lord." Mental assent is not sufficient when it comes to the subject of forgiveness, nor are the mere feelings of regret, even if tears accompany them. Heartfelt emotion, however sincere, is not sufficient either. Forgiveness is not a decision of our will. We may say, "I choose to forgive them, Lord," but still harbor hurt in our souls.

Forgiveness is not an action of our mind, emotions, or will alone, although these faculties are involved. The reality of true forgiveness is this: forgiveness is a Person. It is an encounter with Someone, a supernatural exchange taking place: Christ Himself for our sin and pain. We cannot forgive in our own power, as hard as we may try. Christ is He who forgives through us. We do not extend forgiveness by ourselves, from ourselves.

Christ the forgiver, who lives inside of us, does all the work. True forgiveness requires encountering Christ the forgiver rather than merely knowing and reciting Scriptures or a doctrine of forgiveness.

## FORGIVENESS IS KNOWING

Jesus prayed to the Father, *"And this is life eternal, that they might **know** Thee the only true God, and Jesus Christ whom Thou hast sent"* (John 17:3 KJV). The Greek word translated "know" in this Scripture and other Scriptures calling us to "know" God is *ginōskō*. This "knowing" is very different from mere head knowledge or a conceptual understanding. It is "knowledge grounded in personal experience."

Likewise, the Hebrew word in the Old Testament is *yada'*, as in *"ye shall know that I am the Lord your God"* (Exod. 16:12 KJV). It also means "to know personally by experience"; and it is also used as a euphemism for marital intimacy.

Knowing Christ, then, must involve personal experience or an encounter. And so it is with knowing Christ as our forgiver. We cannot have mere head knowledge of Him being our forgiver, but we must know by experience that He forgives us and extends that forgiveness through us.

A husband and wife had a prayer appointment with Jennifer and me a few years ago. When we asked the wife to tell us where she needed to apply forgiveness, she smiled and said, "Oh, I have forgiven everyone in my life!"

Her husband looked at her in astonishment and said, "Well, what about your sister and our neighbor? What about forgiving our son for not coming home for Thanksgiving? Or forgiving your mother for always criticizing you, and...?"

If you feel *any measure* of unpleasant emotion when you think of or visualize *any* person or situation, present or past, then you still need to experience Christ the forgiver. Ask yourself a few questions: Do I feel hurt because of what someone did to me in the past? Do I feel angry about an injustice done to me? Do I feel intimidated or afraid in certain situations? Do I put up a "wall" in my gut when I think of certain friends or family members?

If you said yes to any of the above, it doesn't mean that you haven't tried to forgive. It just means that your experience of Christ the forgiver needs to become personal and experiential. You're not yet emotionally free. It takes complete forgiveness, not partial forgiveness, to deal with these emotions once and for all.

Forgiveness is not only required for major emotional traumas and injustices, but also for small, everyday irritations and minor offenses we still carry from yesteryear. None of us have resolved every hurt, anger, and fear that has happened from childhood through adulthood, but Christ Himself can and will bring to mind old judgments and bitter roots, quickly replacing them with His presence.

Forgiveness is extremely practical for everyday life—a forgiveness lifestyle. And it's an extremely easy lifestyle to acquire. Jesus Christ is freely available and easily accessible. Forgiveness may *begin* with a thought, choice, or feeling, but it must *end* with a *God encounter*. Although we as believers are called upon to forgive, true and complete forgiveness—with lasting results—is divine, not human. It's supernatural, not natural. It's beyond our human ability: it is the grace and desire of Jesus Christ flowing through us.

## FORGIVENESS DEFINED

Many of us have been taught a wrong view of forgiveness. We somehow equate it with being a doormat or excusing a person of their responsibility in a situation. When we forgive, we are not pardoning in the sense of removing any consequences for their sin or absolving another's sin. We are not pretending to forget about what happened or reconciling with a person when boundaries still need to be established. We are not releasing them from responsibility.

But what we are doing is canceling the debt that was committed against us. We are ceasing to sit in the place of judgment and releasing them to God. If forgiveness is a Person, then it is Christ working through us by His grace to release the wrong done against us. Yes, it includes the mind, will, and emotions, and it must be engaged in with our whole heart.

But forgiveness not only cancels the debt against us, but it frees us through the process as well. When we let Christ forgive through us, we are allowing freedom into our own lives so we will not be poisoned. We are releasing others so that God can work in their lives as well.

It is not an option to forgive, but a command. We must forgive just as God forgave us in Christ. Paul reminds the Ephesians of this when he writes: *"And be kind to one another, tenderhearted, forgiving one another, even as God in Christ forgave you"* (Eph. 4:32).

## FORGIVENESS IS REQUIRED

Most Christians know that forgiving others is commanded by the Word of God, but how many of us still harbor small resentments throughout the day? Forgiveness is not optional, even for minor issues. If we do not forgive others, the Bible says, God will not forgive us: *"But if ye forgive not men their trespasses, neither will your Father forgive your trespasses"* (Matt. 6:15 KJV). It is only if we forgive others that our Father will forgive us (see Matt. 6:14). That doesn't mean that we are condemned to hell if we don't forgive. It only means that we have to live with the torment of our own unforgiveness.

Jesus already paid the penalty for our sin of unforgiveness. Forgiveness releases us and others to God so that He can work in our lives. In other words, when we allow Christ to forgive through us, we cease to sit in the place of judgment:

we release ourselves and others to God, the most just and merciful Judge of the universe.

## THE GRACE OF FORGIVENESS

Even though forgiveness is required of us, it doesn't mean that we do it in our own power or strength. The truth is that Christ forgives through us, but He only does it by grace. We've been taught that grace is the unmerited favor of God. This is only partly true. Grace is so much more than that. It is actually the divine influence upon our life and its reflection in our heart.

Grace is actually the personal presence of Christ empowering us to be all that He has called us to be and to do all that He has called us to do. We forgive, then, by the grace of God. Christ Himself does the forgiving through us—He does all the work as we allow Him access to our hearts. And though it may seem hard to forgive someone for all the hurt they've caused us, it is easy for Him.

## FAILING TO FORGIVE IS DEADLY

A recent Gallup poll indicates that 80 percent of workers feel anxious and stressed out at work. Approximately 18.1 million adults (13.3 percent of the adult U.S. population between 18–54 years old) suffer from anxiety disorders and panic attacks. And the stress is taking its toll on the national health.[1] Studies estimate that 75–90 percent of all doctor's office visits are from stress-related illnesses and complaints. Stress has become a worldwide plague.

What is at the root of this terrible trend? Unforgiveness. Stress isn't inflicted upon us, but arises when we desire to control circumstances or people out of fear, guilt, shame, anger, or hurts.[2] The root of these toxic emotions is unforgiveness toward others, ourselves, or God. The need to control arises when we doubt God's faithfulness and care, or when we hold unforgiveness in our heart.

Medical research now affirms that toxic emotions can make us physically sick. In a 2007 *Journal of the American Medical Association (JAMA)* article, researchers from Carnegie Mellon University and the University of British Columbia examined evidence linking the toxic emotion of stress to increased depression, cardiovascular disease, and the progression of HIV/AIDS.[3]

Studies link emotional distress to six leading causes of death: heart disease and increased risk for heart attack, cancer, lung ailments, accidents, cirrhosis of the liver, and suicide. Research links many health issues with emotions and stress.[4] Some conditions associated with or aggravated by stress include:

| | |
|---|---|
| Back pain | Chronic fatigue |
| Colitis | Crohn's disease |
| Diminished sexual desire | Rosacea, eczema, and psoriasis |
| Headaches | High blood pressure and stroke |
| Irritable bowel syndrome (IBS) | Lowered immune system |
| Peptic ulcers | |

Suppressing emotions has negative consequences on health.[5] Research has indicated that chronic anger and hostility may indeed lead to early death. A long-term study showed that people who score in the high range on hostility scales were almost five times more likely to die of heart disease than those scoring lower. They were also seven times more likely to die by age 50.[6]

The human body is equipped with a protection system for emergency action in dangerous situations. The body responds by releasing stress hormones for "fight or flight" and an instant burst of strength and endurance. Periodic stress does not harm the body, but ongoing *chronic stress* causes lasting damage.[7] Chronic stress overexposes the body to cortisol and other stress hormones, disrupting the function of the immune system, endocrine system, metabolism, cardiovascular system, and nervous system.

The stress of negative emotions can also lead directly to disease. Shortly after Dennis and I were married, I was jerked awake out of a sound sleep by a rapidly racing and pounding heartbeat and a cold sweat. I knew exactly what was happening—paroxysmal atrial tachycardia (PAT). PAT consists of extremely rapid heartbeats that begin and end abruptly. The heart rate suddenly shoots upward to 140–220 beats a minute, and feels like it simply won't slow down.

My heart was beating so fast that it felt as if the bed were shaking. This was not a new thing, but a symptom that had tormented me several times a month for the previous 20 years. Dennis woke up and felt fear flooding the room. I felt fear in my gut but also felt fear all around us in the room. He helped me yield to Christ the forgiver. Instantly, I felt the fear in my gut change to peace, the fear in the room left in a flash, and my heart immediately stopped palpitating, and returned to a gentle, normal rhythm. The atrial tachycardia never recurred again.

The link between stress, anger, fear, and disease is not a new discovery—but few experts know how to instantly and permanently heal toxic emotions. If we don't deal with stress and negative emotions in our lives, they lodge in our cellular memory, stored like toxic waste in a landfill. Suppressed negative emotions don't go away—they are just hidden away under the surface of our conscious awareness.

## FORGIVENESS IS PROVEN

Whereas the terrible consequences of unforgiveness are life-threatening, the tremendous benefits of forgiveness are life-giving. Not only does forgiveness free us from being stuck in the past, but it also brings profound healing to our heart and great clarity to our mind. We are then able to make better decisions based on peace, not anxiety. Forgiveness not only removes barriers that stunt emotional growth, but also spurs intellectual growth: research has proven that stress and anxiety measurably lower your IQ!

Forgiveness results in wellness not only of our souls but also of our bodies. Yielding to Christ the forgiver washes the poison of toxic emotions from our cellular memory and allows physical healing to take place. We have witnessed many hundreds of Christians experience physical healings as they forgive others, themselves, and even the Lord Himself.

John wrote, *"If we confess our sins, He is faithful and just to forgive us our sins and to cleanse us from all unrighteousness"* (1 John 1:9). The Greek word translated "cleanse" here is *katharizō,* which suggests not only moral cleansing but also physical cleansing—the same term used for a leper cleansed of disease.

Forgiveness may be the best medicine ever discovered by science. Since the 1990s, scientific research in the field of forgiveness has exploded, with many scientific studies affirming its physical and psychological benefits. Studies focus on the emotional, mental, and physical benefits of forgiveness as well as the relational and societal implications. Laboratory results document how forgiveness lowers blood pressure, relieves stress, alleviates insomnia, lessens fatigue, and leads to better overall health. Many physicians, therapists, and researchers—both Christian and secular— are turning to forgiveness for answers.

Forgiveness is the God-tool that eradicates stress and toxic emotions, heals our bodies, and ushers us into God-emotions that arise through communion with Christ.

## Forgiveness Is Simple

Based on our own observations over the years, it appears that 90–99 percent of Christians do not know how to forgive properly, effectively, and deliberately so that lingering negative emotions are healed permanently. As a result of lingering resentments and fears, we have difficulty experiencing the presence of God. Even if some Christians occasionally succeed at forgiving and find emotional freedom, they don't know what they did or how they did it—and they cannot teach forgiveness to others.

Most Christians admit that they take a long time to forgive, and justify the delay by ascribing to the erroneous doctrine that forgiveness is a process, not instantaneous. Unfortunately, many Bible scholars and preachers have taught that forgiveness often takes a long time. But consider this: was salvation a process or was it instantaneous? As soon as you repented and asked Christ to be your Lord and Savior, He came into your heart. Jesus was immediately faithful to His Word without delay.

When you received forgiveness from Him, you didn't have to fast and plead. When you were born again, you didn't have to work for forgiveness or beg God for it, you simply received it with childlike faith. You simply opened the door of your heart and received instantaneous forgiveness as a free gift.

Experiencing forgiveness in our daily lives follows exactly the same course: we call to a Person who answers immediately and cleanses us. When we received Christ as our Lord and Savior, we opened our heart to Him and instantly experienced salvation, which was accompanied by peace or joy. And so it is with encountering Christ the forgiver: He *instantly* replaces pain with His peace—with no process required.

This is why Paul wrote to the Colossians:

> *As you have therefore received Christ...[so] walk (regulate your lives and conduct yourselves) in union with and conformity to Him* (Colossians 2:6 AMP).

The word "walk," translated from the Greek *peripateō*, means the way we live everyday life, how we regulate and conduct ourselves and our circumstances. The way we received Christ—calling on Him and receiving His response immediately—defines a lifestyle, the way we walk moment by moment. We call to Him by faith and He responds.

Could it be that the doctrine that promotes forgiveness as a process originated because we just didn't know how to forgive? When we know how to forgive the right way, the process is immediate and permanent, just like our salvation.

Learning how to forgive is vital to every believer, no matter our age, experience, or maturity in the Lord. Even as mature Christians, most of us still carry wounds and offenses from childhood, family and career disappointments, or just daily annoyances, losing God's peace at least occasionally. If we learn to submit every offense to Christ the forgiver, we're guaranteed to find freedom from emotional pain and learn to abide with the Prince of Peace.

The first step in learning how to encounter the forgiver is to locate our emotions, thoughts, will, and heart so we can then yield them to God in exchange for His own.

## NOTES

1.   M. Larzelere and G. Jones, "Stress and health," *Primary Care: Clinics in Office Practice* 35.4 (2008): 839-56.

2.   E. L. Worthington Jr., J. Berry, and L. Parrot III, "Unforgiveness, forgiveness, religion, and health," in T. G. Plante and A. C. Sherman (Editors), *Faith and Health: Psychological Perspectives*, 1st ed. (New York: Guilford Press, 2001), 107-38. K. Lawler, J. Younger, R. Piferi, E. Billington, R. Jobe, K. Edmondson, and W. Jones, "A change of heart: cardiovascular correlates of forgiveness in response to interpersonal conflict," *Journal of Behavioral Medicine* 26 (2003): 373-93. Ibid., "The unique effects of forgiveness on health: an exploration of pathways," *Journal of Behavioral Medicine* 28 (2005): 157-67.

3.   D. Cohen, D. Janicki-Deverts, and G. Miller, "Psychological stress and disease," *Journal of the American Medical Association (JAMA)* 298.14 (2007): 1,685-87.

4.  M. Jensen, "Psychobiological factors predicting the course of breast cancer," *Journal of Personality* 55 (1987): 317-42. M. Larzelere and G. Jones, "Stress and health," *Primary Care: Clinics in Office Practice* 35.4 (2008): 839-856. J. Pennebaker, "Inhibition as the linchpin of health," in H. S. Friedman (Editor), *Hostility, Coping, and Health* (Washington: American Psychological Association, 1992), 127-39. L. Temoshok, "Personality, coping style, emotion, and cancer: Toward an integrative model, " *Cancer Surveys* 6 (1987): 545-67. L. Dennerstein, P. Lehert, H. Burger, and E. Dudley, "Factors affecting sexual functioning of women in the mid-life years," *Climacteric* 2 (1999): 254–62.

5.  J. Gross and R. Levenson, "Hiding feelings: The acute effects of inhibiting positive and negative emotions," *Journal of Abnormal Psychology* 106 (1997): 95-103. J. Pennebaker, "Inhibition as the linchpin of health," in H. S. Feidman (Editor), *Hostility, Coping, and Health*, (Washington: American Psychological Association, 1992), 127-139.

6.  J. Barefoot et al., "Hostility CHD Incidence in Total Mortality—A Twenty-Five Year Follow-Up Study of Twenty-Five Physicians," *Psychosomatic Medicine* (1984): 45:79-83.

7.   A. Baum and D. Polsusnzy, "Health Psychology: Mapping Biobehavioral Contributions to Health and Illness," *Annual Review of Psychology*, col. 50, (199): 137-163. N. B. Anderson and P. E. Anderson, *Emotional Longevity: What Really Determines How Long You Live* (New York: Viking, 2002). A. N. Vgontzas et al., "Chronic insomnia and activity of the stress system: a preliminary study," *Journal of Psychosomatic Research*, vol. 45 (1997): 21-31.

# Chapter 5

# LOCATION, LOCATION, LOCATION

## TOO MUCH IN THE HEAD

The number one rule in real estate is *location, location, location*. This same principle applies to spiritual growth as well. Many Christians struggle with forgiveness and communion with God because they don't understand their spiritual real estate; they don't understand where their spiritual heart resides.

Understanding the inner-workings of our emotions, thoughts, will, and heart is the first step in learning to meet Christ the forgiver. I (Dennis) had a 30-day visitation of the Lord in which God taught me about how to be in

His presence seven days a week, 24 hours a day, when I was first saved. He taught me how to walk in such peace that no circumstance could ever take it away, unless I temporarily gave in to a negative emotion. But through forgiveness, peace is always instantly restored. The Lord once told me, "Don't ever let anything come between what you and I have together!" This, biblically speaking, is normal Christianity. It has to start with location.

We have to know the location of our heart, or where our spirit resides. If the Holy Spirit lives within us, then we have to let Him rule and reign within us as well. But if we don't know where our heart resides, and I'm not talking about our physical heart here, then how can we be aware of what He is doing if we're not focusing on the right place?

When any person or situation comes into our lives, causing us distress, then we'll lose our peace. But if we don't know where that peace resides, how will we know if we lost it or not? If we're paying attention to the right place we'll feel the peace leave the moment that situation arises. We're often too cerebral, paying too much attention to our rational thoughts instead of our heart. And by no means does God want us to throw our brains away—but He does want us to be tuned into our spirits.

So we want to spend time in this chapter helping us locate our emotions, our spiritual hearts, our will, and our thoughts. That way we'll be better prepared to know when Christ is ruling and reigning within, and when we have stepped into the realm of the flesh.

## LOCATE OUR SPIRITUAL HEART (EMOTIONS)

Most people associate the chest cavity with their emotional life and spiritual center, and try to live out their Christianity from just behind their breastbone. Somehow we have mistaken the Hallmark version of the red Valentine heart for the seat of love, affection, and the Spirit of God.

The Bible does not locate our spiritual and emotional centers within our chest, however, but in the area of our belly. This may seem strange—or just a minor detail or mere semantics—but the location of our spiritual and emotional core matters greatly in learning how to use the God-tool of supernatural forgiveness.

Scripture is very clear about where our emotional center is positioned. The Hebrew term *me'ah* and the Greek *splagchnon,* both translated "bowels," refer not only to the physical digestive organs but also to the location of our emotions, whether they are feelings of distress, tenderness, mercy, or love. This is our Bible heart, the seat of our emotions. (This doesn't mean our spiritual heart resides in a physical organ of the body. It just pinpoints the epicenter of emotional and spiritual experience.)

The heart is the center of a person's inward life, the sphere of divine influence. Whenever the Bible talks about the heart, it is not referring to the natural heart. Consider the use of the term "bowels" in the following Scriptures:

*I am poured out like water, and all my bones are out of joint: my heart is like wax; it is melted in the midst of my **bowels** (Psalm 22:14 KJV).*

*Mine eyes do fail with tears, my **bowels** are troubled (Lamentations 2:11 KJV).*

*If there be therefore any consolation in Christ, if any comfort of love, if any fellowship of the Spirit, if any **bowels** and mercies... (Philippians 2:1 KJV).*

*Put on therefore, as the elect of God, holy and beloved, **bowels** of mercies, kindness, humbleness of mind, meekness, longsuffering (Colossians 3:12 KJV).*

*But whoso hath this world's good, and seeth his brother have need, and shutteth up his **bowels** of compassion from him, how dwelleth the love of God in him? (1 John 3:17 KJV)*

Clearly, the area of our bowels is the location of compassion, mercy, kindness, humility, meekness, and long-suffering—even despair.

Other Hebrew and Greek words referring to our spiritual heart are translated as "belly." This belly region comprises the location of God's Spirit within us, from which the life of God is released. This can be seen in both the Old and New Testaments. The spirit of man is said to reside in the belly: *"The spirit of man is the lamp of the Lord, searching all the* *inward parts of the **belly***" (Prov. 20:27 KJV). The anointing from Christ flows from the belly: *"He that believeth on Me, as the scripture hath said, out of his **belly** shall flow rivers of living water"* (John 7:38 KJV).

According to the Bible, then, our spiritual heart or inner-most being is not located in our chest, but at our mid-section, within the belly. Our Bible heart is located within our bellies.

## LOCATE OUR WILL

Most of us will be surprised to learn that our belly or gut is not only the seat of our spirit and emotions, but also of our conscience, intention, and will—the faculties of choice and decision making. Willpower, self-discipline, and self-control are among the most misunderstood and misapplied concepts in the Christian life—leading to a "faith walk" governed by striving, pride, and self-effort. Understanding the location of our will and how to yield our will are two of the most pow-erful lessons we can ever learn as followers of Christ.

The word *will,* in some translations of the Old Testament, is translated "reins," or literally our "kidneys" (see Jer. 17:10 KJV). Our will, that uniquely human faculty of choice and volition, is in our gut—not, as many believe, in our mind, in the brain between our ears.

Are you unclear about the location of your will? Pay attention the next time a minor inconvenience or offense occurs. You will notice that your gut muscles tighten. You have erected a protective wall to guard your heart and exert your own will. If you keep that wall up between you and the person or situation, you will begin to feel stress and anxiety, lose your peace, and you may even notice that the muscular tension increases and spreads—to your back, shoulders, and neck. This is your willpower at work, trying to control a threatening situation, defend yourself, or keep others at a distance.

### Practice

*Try this simple exercise to locate your will. Stand up and allow yourself to fall back a little, but stop yourself before falling. (You may want to try this with your back against a wall.) Where do you feel the stop? You will feel your belly or gut tighten. You stopped yourself as an action of your will. Your volition, or will, is activated in your belly, together with your heart.*

*Now close your eyes and think of an unpleasant person or stressful situation. Pay attention to what you sense in your gut. Notice the increase in tension. Your will actively resists the unpleasant encounter by erecting an invisible wall to protect yourself. And all of this takes place in your belly.*

## LOCATE OUR THOUGHTS

You think thoughts in your head, of course, but you also have "thoughts" in your heart. Have you ever heard someone describe a "hunch" or "gut" reaction? Have you ever felt a "knowing" in your gut that you couldn't really explain with your brain? We can often find wisdom when we "go with our gut" when making decisions, relying on more than just logic and analysis.

The validity of "gut instincts" is now proven by laboratory research. Scientists and therapists document that our gut, bowels, or belly region is the place not only of emotion and will, but is also inseparable from cognition or thought. We have *feeling-thoughts*, or "emo-cognitions."

Recent research confirms that we have an emotional "brain" in our gut that is as active and important as the brain between our ears. Dr. Michael Gershon calls it the "second brain."[1] Experts in neurobiology and psychotherapy have since defined a new field of research, *neurogastroenterology* or "enteric neurology."

Although we have a brain between our ears, God has given us a "second brain" with an equally significant function of cognition in our gut. Have you ever heard anyone use the expression "I know that I know"? There are two places of knowing: the brain between our ears and the second brain, called the "enteric nervous system."

There are as many neurons in the enteric nervous system as there are in the brain and central nervous system. Millions of neurons line the walls of our esophagus, intestines, stomach, and colon. Our two brains interact by way of the "left vagus nerve," connecting the emotional center in the brain (the limbic system) directly to the intestines. Neuropeptides, molecules of emotion, are released throughout the body and brain, transmitting emotional information to every cell, organ, and system of the entire body.

We can witness the validity of "gut responses" in a new type of polygraph test. The traditional polygraph assessment collects physiological data from at least three systems in the human body, including respiratory activity, sweat gland activity, and cardiovascular activity. Unfortunately, it is possible to beat a polygraph. There is plenty of information out there teaching people how to do just that.

Dr. Pankaj Pasricha and his team at the University of Texas recently measured nerve activity in the stomachs of volunteers, asking some individuals to lie and others to tell the truth.[2] Those who lied were discovered by measuring reactions in the gut. Dr. Pasricha observed, "The gut has a mind of its own. Its nervous system acts independently." In other words, this is a polygraph system that is completely reliable. In 2008, Dr. Pasricha applied for a patent for a new type of lie detector based on his research.[3]

Now we can understand why we immediately feel an emotion, often in our belly area, when we think about a painful experience or imagine a hurtful person. Our two "brains" are experiencing the memory at the exact same time. It is as important to attend to the thoughts or images in our head as it is to feel the emotions in our "bowels." Suppressing negative emotions associated with thoughts only buries them deeper in our unconscious, making communion with Christ more difficult. Christ the forgiver wants to cleanse toxic emotions from every cell and every neural pathway.

## LOCATE WHAT OR WHO IS RULING

If our own soul rules, we will think our own thoughts, feel our own feelings, and choose to do our own will every time. But if we yield to Christ within, His thoughts will become our thoughts, His feelings will be our feelings, and His will becomes our will. In other words, God's revelations will rule over our mind. The conviction and direction of the Holy Spirit will guide our will. And Christ's heart will transform our emotions to be His own.

Paul reminds us, *"Let the peace of God rule in your hearts"* (Col. 3:15). He desires to rule over every part of our being so we can be set apart for the Lord. This is the process known as sanctification: we are progressively letting Christ rule and reign over us, submitting more areas of our life to Him, a little more each day, thus becoming more like Him on an ongoing basis.

Many Christians attempt sanctification in the wrong manner. In an effort to renew our minds and calm our troubled emotions, we try to push or force-feed the Bible from our head to our heart, and often call this process "meditating on the Word." Most believers will admit that this process is ineffective, despite our good intentions. We may know the Bible "by heart" and earnestly quote Scriptures about peace and joy to renew our mind, yet we may still battle stress, anxiety, and fear, harboring resentment and tossing at night.

Antidepressants and cognitive or behavioral therapies are popular secular alternatives for emotional healing, and may indeed be somewhat effective for a season. But the root issues of the spiritual being will remain unchanged.

Willfully changing our minds or habits through talk therapy or self-discipline, or altering brain chemistry through drugs may alleviate or lessen our symptoms and offer much-needed relief—if not life-saving intervention—but ultimately only Christ the forgiver will bring permanent freedom, peace, and joy. Only Christ Himself can bring new life to a broken soul, and the life of Christ flows out from our innermost being—not our minds or by our willpower.

Paul wrote about the need for us to renew our minds so we will know the will of God:

> *And do not be conformed to this world, but be transformed by the renewing of your mind, that you may prove what is that good and acceptable and perfect will of God* (Romans 12:2).

The Greek term *nous*, translated "mind" here, is more accurately rendered "mindset," which includes the entire soul—the thoughts, will, and emotions—or our ability to think, choose, and feel. In other words, our entire soul needs to be transformed, not just our cognitive processes or thoughts.

In order to be transformed in the biblical sense, we need to have a renewed soul. We must face and feel every emotion that arises, without denial or avoidance, to give the Lord the opportunity to bless that emotion as honoring Him, or cleanse that emotion as a wound in our soul. The Holy Spirit will transform our soul as we yield to the Spirit of Christ within.

Some Christian teachings wrongly encourage us to disregard or subdue our emotions by sheer willpower alone, or by applying the Word of God to our situation. On the contrary, paying keen attention to negative emotions, as painful as they are, is an essential part of abiding in Christ and practicing the presence of God. Once we learn the secret of releasing forgiveness, we'll see negative emotions as marvelous opportunities to experience Christ the forgiver all over again. We must allow our emotions to become our friends. They tell us whether or not Christ is ruling at any given moment. When He rules our lives, we feel peace.

It's important to remember that there are no big or little offenses to forgive. No matter the severity or history of the issue, every wound is easy for Jesus to heal. Some believers feel that sanctification—our soul being set apart for Christ—is not necessary. Or, if it is, that it is a sovereign work of God that has nothing to do with us.

But on the contrary, sanctification must be intentional. The Bible exhorts us to *"be ye transformed by the renewing"* of our soul (Romans 12:2 KJV), which suggests that it is our responsibility as Christians to participate. How do we collaborate with God in intentional sanctification without exerting our willpower, striving, or trying to be holy?

The next important step to learn is the easiest "how to" of all: we must learn how to yield, to drop down, and welcome Christ the forgiver to do His sanctifying work in our souls.

---

### Practice

*Close your eyes in prayer and focus on Christ within. Notice how it feels when you pay attention to the Lord. Stay focused on Him a while longer. Notice how different this feels from being stressed. God longs for you to live with a conscious awareness of Him every day.*

---

## Notes

1.   M. Gershon, *The Second Brain* (New York, NY: HarperCollins, 1999).

2.   S. Hutson, "Gut reactions may rumble a liar," *New Scientist* 31 (October 2005): http://www.newscientist.com/article/dn8238-gut-reactions-may-rumble-a-liar.html (accessed January 8, 2012).

3.   "Patent: Checking your gut to see if you lie," *Texas Business* 29 (December 2011): http://www.texasbusiness.com/patent-checking-your-gut-to-see-if-you-lie--cms-6681 (accessed January 8, 2012).

Chapter 6

# DROPPING DOWN

## PAY ATTENTION

Most Christians focus their conscious attention either in their head, conducting their relationship with God in their thought life, or in their chest area, living from their carnal emotions. But if our spirit-heart resides in our belly—not between our ears or within our chest—then we need to refocus our conscious attention. We need to shift our focus away from our head and chest, and down to our true spirit being within our belly. We call this shift of conscious attention "dropping down." We originally coined the term "drop down" the first year we were married. I often found it necessary to remind Jen to practice dropping down from her head to her heart during the day, whenever she started analyzing or worrying about something.

By dropping down, we pay attention to our belly area—a subtle but ever-so-powerful change of focus. Dropping down shifts our focus from our head to our heart. This refocusing of awareness is absolutely vital to our communion with God. Without this shift in attention, we can remain detached from our spirit, living our Christian life through our intellect or carnal emotions alone.

Only as we locate our spirit-heart correctly can we guard our heart, as Proverbs 4:23 instructs us, *"for out of it spring the issues of life."* The Hebrew word *leb* used in this Proverb, translated "heart," occurs almost 600 times throughout the Old Testament. It is very general, referring to many aspects of our being, including our mind, will, understanding, soul, memory, passions, and the place where we feel courage.

According to the New Testament, the heart at our core is also where our conscience resides, together with the center of our emotions, moral nature, and spiritual life—which, as we have learned in John 7:38, flows out of the belly.

Within our heart, we locate the following:

- The seat of grief (see John 14:1; Rom. 9:2; 2 Cor. 2:4).

- Joy (see John 16:22; Eph. 5:19).

- The desires (see Matt. 5:28; 2 Pet. 2:14).

- The affections (see Luke 24:32; Acts 21:13).

- The perceptions (see John 12:40; Eph. 4:18).

- The thoughts (see Matt. 9:4; Heb. 4:12).

- The understanding (see Matt. 13:15; Rom. 1:21).

- The reasoning powers (see Mark 2:6; Luke 24:38).

- The imagination (see Luke 1:51).

- The conscience (see Acts 2:37; 1 John 3:20).

- The intentions (see Heb. 4:12; 1 Pet. 4:1).

- Purpose (see Acts 11:23; 2 Cor. 9:7).

- The will (see Rom. 6:17; Col. 3:15).

- Faith (see Mark 11:23; Rom. 10:10; Heb. 3:12).

As we can see, the belly is the location of our entire emotional and spiritual heart-life. The wounds of our heart are also located in the area of our gut, not in our chest. Although we may sometimes feel emotional heartache inside our chest cavity, jerk when startled, or get red-faced with embarrassment, the epicenter of the damage is in the belly. The writer of Proverbs says it this way: *"The words of a talebearer are as wounds, and they go down into the innermost parts of the belly"* (Prov. 18:8 KJV).

> ### *Practice*
>
> *Close your eyes and think of an unpleasant person or situation, current or past. Pay attention to how it feels in your gut. Now think of a good memory. How does that feel? Can you name the emotion?*

By dropping down and refocusing our conscious awareness from our head and chest area to our belly region, we immediately gain a greater sense not only of our emotions and spirit but also of the Spirit of Christ Himself, who lives within us.

## STEPS TO DROPPING DOWN

Let me give you a real-life example of dropping down. Let's say you are walking in peace all day long and you think you're just having the time of your life. You go to the local grocery store, and coming down the aisle the other way is your "enemy," the neighbor who has continually been difficult to deal with. This is someone who really has it in for you; someone that's done you harm in the past—and they're walking right toward you. A one-time situation is easy to resolve, but an ongoing problem requires a little more perseverance.

The way we normally behave, even as Christians, is that we automatically put up a wall in our spirits. If we don't turn around and go the other way before he sees us, then we think, *Oh, there's Ralph coming down the aisle. He's already seen me, so there's no use turning around and going the other way. Well, I guess I have to talk to him.* But unconsciously, we only listen to him with our heads. We put a wall up in our heart, and the door of our heart becomes closed to him.

And then we mistakenly believe that this is the normal Christian life, it is the natural way to live. But it's not. It is something that is fleshly. The normal way to live, under the authority of Christ, is that when we see Ralph coming, we drop down into our spiritual heart and feel Christ's peace ruling there. When His peace is ruling, the Scripture takes place as an experience: the *"peace of God...will guard your hearts and your minds through Christ Jesus"* (Phil. 4:7).

The second step, then, is that when we feel a negative emotion coming from our gut when we first see Ralph, we present it to Christ within us. It is not sinful to feel the emotion, but it is God revealing pain and hurt in our life that He wants to heal. So as we yield to the forgiver within us, we let Him go to that feeling and through that feeling. It's like Jesus walked through the walls of our heart and took away the toxic emotions that dwelt there. It is a supernatural exchange taking place and the negative emotions suddenly turn to peace. It is not a natural peace we can think up with our minds, but a supernatural one that passes our understanding and cognitive faculties.

There are many Christians living in sin and still claim they feel the peace of God with their lifestyle. But we could show them a test to find out if it is really peace they are experiencing. Because the truth is that there is a lot of false peace in the world today. False peace means, "I'm doing what I want to do and I have peace about it"—it is as if we have to take their word for it. But if they are willing to listen, we could simply tell them that there's a hardness that is discernible in their "peace." In other words, they can say no so many times that they desensitize themselves to the Holy Spirit and their consciences become seared.

But a person of faith can be in their presence and the love of God can "melt" that hardness so they can feel the presence of the true peace once again. This is what we call displacement. If we have peace ruling in our heart and you have hardness of heart, we could release the love of God to you so that even on the hardness of heart, conviction could be stirred up again.

The third step would be that when we forgive, we know that there is a growing internal strength to deal with whatever area that was recurring with that person. Say we run into Ralph regularly all around town. We notice that when we first saw him, we were devastated. But we dropped down and allowed Christ's peace to change our negative emotions.

The next time we see Ralph, we notice that we are only mildly irritated with him this time. So we let Christ work within us once again. Then, when we run into him the third time, it's like water rolling off our back. It's like we don't feel any negative emotion at all—it has been displaced by the peace of God. That means we are growing in our spiritual prowess.

The fruit of patience is being formed within us as we go through this process. Patience is holding the heart open but getting stronger in the spirit all the time. So when we face repetitive situations, we are actually growing stronger in the anointing of displacement. Christ is ruling and reigning in our heart a little more each time we yield to Him and drop down.

## Practical Application

Let's say someone has offended you deeply. You have chosen to forgive him, and you have even willed to forgive him. But you feel churning in your gut anytime his name is brought up. How do you get rid of that feeling? How do you truly forgive that individual?

The easiest way to do this is to put your hand on your belly. Picture the person who offended you. Feel the negative emotion in your gut. When the person comes to your mind, there is a corresponding emotion present. This happens every time, no exceptions.

That emotion resides where your hand is right now, whether you can specifically name it or not. But we do know it is not the fruit of the Spirit—*"love, joy, peace, longsuffering, kindness, goodness, faithfulness, gentleness, self-control"* (Gal.

5:22-23). So there is something between you and them as long as you feel that negative emotion. When that negative emotion is replaced by peace, then you know that Christ the forgiver has done His work and they are truly forgiven.

With your hand now on your belly, allow Christ the forgiver to go to that negative wall of emotion and go through it. He carries that negative emotion off on a river of loving, living water—it's loving forgiveness that flows out of our belly; it usually only takes seconds for it to change to peace for most people. When you can picture that person in your head and feel peace down in your heart, you have a historical record in your head but a heavenly record in your gut that you are clean and forgiven.

### *Abusive Relationship*

There was an 18-year-old girl that was stuck in an abusive relationship that she felt was manipulative and controlling. She was frustrated and wanted to be free of it. So she asked her parents, who were pastors, if she could fly down and have a session with me (Dennis). They allowed her. When she arrived at my office, she said, "You taught me how to do this, but I'm struggling. I've got this relationship that I'm in, and I don't want to hate those involved." She basically just wanted to release forgiveness to all involved.

And that made perfect sense to me, because at that point of asking how to break free, I said, "Receive forgiveness for opening up an emotional attachment to that individual.

Receive forgiveness for opening up to a relationship that wasn't godly. Your emotions belong to God, and He wants to heal those."

She received forgiveness, but she also needed the attachment with them to be broken. I said, "You belong to Christ within. He is your Lord; therefore, even your mind, will, and your emotions belong to Him." And she let Christ flow through her, and He brought healing to her soul.

When she allowed Him to flow through her, she made a comment to me afterward that has stuck with me ever since. She said, "I don't have to hate them, but the pull is no longer there; the pull, the force of lustful attraction, or even the need to be with that individual is no longer there." Suddenly that attraction was broken through the peace of Christ.

### Contrary Circumstances

Dropping down works for any circumstance that we could ever possibly find ourselves in. Maybe you've just lost your job, or you don't have money to pay your mortgage. You are in absolute turmoil. Maybe you're about to lose your house. And so you ask, "How can I be activated in peace?"

What you can do is eliminate the torment in the midst of a bad situation. You simply drop down to the negative emotion you're feeling about that specific situation, and you allow Christ to release forgiveness through you toward anyone you are upset with, God or other people. Receive forgiveness for taking in any fear. Then, release the circumstances into the hands of God. Yield to Him, allowing Him to replace that emotion with His peace in your heart.

Each of us have the capacity to yield to God even in the midst of the worst circumstances. He can give us at least the peace of knowing that He's in charge, He's ruling everything around us. And even before we have an answer, the torment goes and is replaced by peace. When God's love is released into a situation, the torment can no longer stand. Even though the circumstances around us haven't changed, our heart is no longer flooded by negative emotions, but by the peace of God.

### *Friends Becoming Enemies*

When we walk in this level of peace, even our enemies can become our friends. There was a young pastor where we lived, and he didn't like or understand some of the things I (Dennis) was teaching. So he decided to write three consecutive articles about me—he didn't name my name, but it fit me so well I knew whom he was talking about. The first time I read the article, it devastated me. I thought I was going to get sick in my stomach. So I released forgiveness and it came to peace, but in the back of my mind I knew article number two was coming next week.

And article two came the following week. It bothered me that time as well, but it wasn't as bad as the first week. Then article three came the third week, and it didn't affect me at all. The love of God was flowing out of me and it was a finished work. I had perfect peace in the midst of this young pastor bashing my teaching and saying false accusations about me. I would see him around town for the next 10 years.

After that time, we were both at a local pastors' meeting when he broke down, sobbing in front of all the pastors. "Ten years ago I personally attacked Dennis Clark," he said. "And he's been nothing but a gentleman to me for ten years." Then he went on: "I want to publicly acknowledge that I love that man. I believe what he's teaching, and I've even been a recipient of it."

God had allowed my enemies to become my friends when I dropped down and let the peace of Christ rule in my heart.

Chapter 7

# THE GRACE OF YIELDING

## YIELDING ACTIVATES GOD'S PRESENCE

Have you ever heard the beautiful hymn "I Surrender All"? It is about the lordship of Jesus Christ—yielding our will to do His will. People used to sing it a lot in church and go to the altar when it was being sung, but few seemed to really understand how to surrender or where to surrender. Most of them probably didn't even know where the will was, much less how to deliberately yield their will to the Lord.

Understanding the location of our will and how to yield our will are two of the most powerful lessons we can ever learn as followers of Christ. Now that we understand the location of the will in our gut, we can learn to yield and allow Christ to flow like a river from our innermost being. Unless this lesson is learned, we will struggle in many areas of our Christian life.

As we drop down and refocus our conscious attention to our belly region, we will begin to discern our emotional state and the condition of our will. We may feel a negative emotion when recalling a painful situation, or we may feel tension in our gut when our will is defending us against a threatening situation or person.

Yielding our will activates Christ's presence within us. We yield, He works. His Spirit indwells every believer and, as we read in Philippians 2:13, *"it is God who is **at work in you**, both **to will** and **to work** for His good pleasure"* (NASB). When we fail to yield to Him, then we are left to our own resources. But if we yield to Him, letting Christ have full reign within, then God works on our behalf.

Christ is near, even in our heart. Distance is only a deception when it comes to the presence of God. God is in heaven, of course, but He is also with us and in us. It is one of the spiritual mysteries that is proclaimed throughout the Bible. Everything we need is found in Christ. He is our treasure, our provider, and our provision. And He is with us every moment of every day. He came as a Savior, but He is also our Immanuel, which means "God with us" (see Matt. 1:23). Paul says that Christ resides within us: *"**Christ in you**, the hope of* *glory"* (Col. 1:27); and Jesus said that the *"kingdom of God is **within you"*** (Luke 17:21).

So how exactly do we yield our will and let Christ within flow out? Jesus said, *"He that believeth on Me, as the scripture hath said, out of his belly shall flow rivers of living water"* (John 7:38 KJV). As soon as we yield our will to God's will, we make a spiritual connection with Him. God's will is not just a plan, but a flow of divine purpose, like a river. We can allow the river to flow to us and through us, or we can just as easily shut it off.

## YIELDING, NOT STRIVING

This is so simple to do. It confounds us because there's an awareness and a presence that is available, and every aspect of God's character and His nature—the fruit of the Spirit— are available to us. In fact, the fruit of the Spirit are in us and they can be applied to the situations of our life. But the important thing is that we don't have to strive to produce them, we simply yield and allow Him to flow through us.

Paul writes:

> *I have been crucified with Christ; it is no longer I who live, but Christ lives in me; and the life which I now live in the flesh I live by faith in the Son of God, who loved me and gave Himself for me. I do not set aside the grace of God; for if righteousness*

*comes through the law, then Christ died in vain*
(Galatians 2:20-21).

The interesting thing about this is that it suggests that Jesus is the forgiver and the deliverer. If it is no longer I who live but Christ who lives in me, then it is no longer I who love but Christ who loves in and through me. Then this also suggests that it is no longer I who forgive but Christ in me who forgives. I have to yield to Him working through me, allowing Him to do the work, giving Him the opportunity to do it. We colabor with Christ.

And this is why Paul wrote to the Philippians, *"For it is God who works in you both to will and to do for His good pleasure"* (Phil. 2:13). As we yield to Christ within, He is the One who wills and works to do His good pleasure. As we yield to Him, He works. As we reach out and touch Him, allowing Him to work, He is the One who works.

That means we're no longer striving in our own good works. The force of supernatural love is the motivation that lifts us into a higher spiritual realm, causing our emotions to be whole, living in a lifestyle of peace and continual communion in His presence. It is truly the *fruit* of the Holy Spirit, not fruit we can produce on our own. It is not us but Christ working through us producing the fruit and doing the forgiving. We have to open our will and allow Him to work, however.

## THE DOOR OF OUR WILL

We open the door to welcome Christ when we are born again; but we must also learn to yield to Christ and allow His Spirit to have dominion in our soul on a daily basis. This comes by opening the door of our hearts continually. Jesus said to the church in Revelation: *"Behold, I stand at the door and knock. If anyone hears My voice and opens the door, I will come in to him and dine with him, and he with Me"* (Rev. 3:20). It has been pointed out that this verse is directed to a church rather than to an individual, but church means "a congregation or assembly" not a building. People, not buildings, open the door of their heart to Jesus.

Imagine hearing a car pull up at your house and seeing your least favorite person walking to your front door. You put up an inner wall in your gut with your will, closing the door of your spiritual heart in order to protect yourself. Your will-power has taken over to control an unpleasant circumstance. So you simply close the door to protect your emotions.

The heart in our belly has a door that gives God and other people access to it or denies them access. And that door to our heart is our will. When we are suspicious about some-one's motives, we close our heart to them and stop being vulnerable: our will shuts the door of our heart. When we feel tension in our gut, we know that our willpower has been engaged. We're willfully closing the door of our hearts.

It is important to remember that we open to Christ within us; we don't open to other people. That way we are still open, but the peace of God is armor for our souls: peace protects our heart and our mind. We are instructed to put on armor, to wear shoes of peace (see Eph. 6:15). When peace is guarding us, it is like having a strong screen door—the fresh air can circulate, we can feel the breeze, but mosquitoes can't come in. Paul confirmed this when he said, *"The peace of God, which surpasses all understanding, will guard your hearts and minds through Christ Jesus"* (Phil. 4:7).

Since Jesus said He stands at the door of our heart and knocks, we can choose whether or not to open the door of our will and connect with love inside—and allow Love Himself to flow out. It's a matter of yielding our will and letting the door swing open. That door is what opens for Jesus when we are saved. It is also the "valve" that can open or shut off the connection with God in the daily life of a believer.

Our relationship with God is not a matter of thinking about the Lord, analyzing Scriptures, or saying mental prayers, but an act of our will to open the door of our heart. Consider what Jesus said about mere head knowledge of Him:

> *You have your heads in your Bibles constantly because you think you'll find eternal life there. But you miss the forest for the trees. These Scriptures are all about Me! And here I am, standing right before you, and you aren't willing to receive from Me the life you say you want* (John 5:39-40 MSG).

The Bible, however, says that God is a spiritual being and those who worship Him must approach Him in spirit and truth (see John 4:24). The connection with God must be made by our spirit, not our intellect alone—our heart not our head! Thinking about God is not the same thing as having an experiential encounter with Him. Jesus said:

> *Your worship must engage your spirit in the pursuit of truth. That's the kind of people the Father is out looking for: those who are simply and honestly themselves before Him in their worship. God is sheer being itself—Spirit. Those who worship Him must do it out of their very being, their spirits, their true selves, in adoration* (John 4:23-24 MSG).

Our will is the door into the spiritual realm. As we yield our will to God, we open a spiritual connection to the presence of God. He lives in our spirit-man, in our innermost being, not in our head or carnal emotions. In order to connect with Him on a spiritual level, the door of our heart must be open so He is allowed to enter in.

## DROP DOWN AND YIELD

We now understand that it's vital to open the door of our heart, which is located in our belly, by yielding our will to Christ. A yielded will opens the heart to Him, allowing Him to come in and set up His abode within us.

Remember the earlier exercise of standing up and letting yourself fall back slightly? When you stopped yourself from falling, you exercised the faculty of your will (in your gut) to control yourself. That same will is what you need to release in order to contact your spirit.

Dropping down to Christ means refocusing your conscious attention away from your head, down into your belly region, to make a spirit connection to Christ. Again, Christ within is not in our chest cavity but in our innermost being, down in the belly area. It is like dropping a bucket down into a well in order to draw up water.

We simply open the door of our heart by relaxing our will. This relaxation feels a bit like relaxing our abdominal muscles: when we relax our will, the door of our heart opens, and living water from Christ within flows out from our spirit. Does this sound too mechanical to be God? Does God really inhabit a certain place in our body? (It is not that God inhabits a physical organ in the body, but there is a *spiritual place* where we encounter His presence.) Let us explain.

The Lord is King over all of us—body, soul, and spirit. But some parts of our being are not yet set apart for His use. This means that they're still wounded and confused, and they filter our experience of God. When we drop down and connect with God in our spirit, focusing on our belly, we are no longer relying on our mind or fleshly emotions to communicate with Christ within or experience His presence. We are rather focusing on Him with our spiritual heart.

The mechanics of dropping down to focus on our spirit is a method for helping believers identify the spirit-faculty given to us by God, through which we worship Him and abide in Christ.

## CONNECT WITH CHRIST WITHIN

As soon as we drop down, we need to yield our will and open the door of our heart. We will instantly make a connection to God in our spirit and feel His peace. When we open the door of our heart, Christ promises to have fellowship with us, no matter what. He is always there when we begin to focus on Him.

If we then start thinking about our to-do list, all the worries and responsibilities of our day, a mild anxiety begins to move in. But as soon as we drop down again and connect with God spirit to Spirit in our belly, the anxiety will leave and peace will again return. All our worries will fade in the light of His presence.

### Practice

*Place your hand on your belly. Drop down and focus on Christ within. Relax your will by leaning back a bit, rocking back on your heels. Or you may want to lean back slightly against a wall. Don't think or try to feel anything. Just be aware of Christ within you.*

*Relax your will, almost like a "cuckoo clock" door opening in your belly. You will immediately notice His presence and His peace coming from deep within you. Bask in His love for a moment.*

Dropping down and yielding our will are skills that can be learned and developed with practice. Once we learn to open to Christ within, the next step is learning how to abide with His peace, His *shalom,* without interruption. This is the place we are made to live.

Chapter 8

# THE PEACE OF GOD

## THE *SHALOM* OF GOD

What is *shalom,* the Hebrew word of the English translation of *peace*? The Hebrew people understood things in total concepts, as pervading all of life. We define peace as the absence of turmoil, but for the Hebrews it was so much more than that. When they used the word *shalom,* they could be saying goodbye or hello, they could be talking about completeness, wholeness, peace, health, prosperity, welfare, safety, salvation, deliverance, tranquility, or a perfectness pervading the whole of human life.

*Shalom* is defined as "nothing separating us." Sin separates us from God, but forgiveness cleanses sin and gives us peace with Him. Likewise, forgiving people removes the walls of separation erected in our hearts, thus making peace with other people. The Hebrews would be talking about a total sense of well-being, where all things were intact and whole.

God's *shalom* is also the absence of conflict—a deep, inner tranquility. It is defined by completeness, safety, health, prosperity, quiet, contentment, and welfare. *Shalom* is the absence of stress, anxiety, fear, resentment, or worry. The Bible clearly states we are not to fear, to cast all of our cares on Him, and not to worry about anything (see Isa. 41:10; 1 Pet. 5:7; Phil 4:6-8).

When Paul was writing to the Philippians, who were overcome with worry, he gave them the remedy—prayer. He said:

> *Don't worry about anything; instead, pray about everything.... Then you will experience God's peace, which exceeds anything we can understand. His peace will guard your hearts and minds as you live in Christ Jesus* (Philippians 4:6-7 NLT).

As soon as we connect to Christ within, internal conflict will dissipate and we will feel peace. Sometimes it is gentle, and at other times it is quite profound.

Peace is extremely practical. As soon as we drop down and yield to His will, we experience a deep and abiding peace in our hearts. God's presence and His peace are available to us at all times, no matter where we are at or what situation we are in. We don't have to be in a prayer closet to drop down and experience peace. We can experience it in the same measure when we're at work, on our commute home, or when our computer crashes.

God's extraordinary peace and the joy that follows are the manifestations of the love of God, described as "the fruit of the Spirit." Paul writes, *"But the fruit of the Spirit is love, joy, peace, longsuffering, kindness, goodness, faithfulness, gentleness, self-control* (temperance)" (Gal. 5:22-23).

These are the emotions of God. We experience God-emotions flowing through our emotions as the fruit of the Spirit. God is an emotional *God*. He doesn't just have love, He is love; He doesn't just have peace, He Himself is peace. He is joy, He is gentleness, and He is faithfulness.

God's peace is the peace that *"surpasses all understanding"* (Phil. 4:7). "Understanding" comes from the Greek word *nous,* which includes thoughts, choices, and emotions. God's supernatural peace is supremely better, higher, and more excellent than anything that comes from our human thinking, choosing, or feeling. Jesus said, *"Peace I leave with you; My peace I give you. I do not give to you as the world gives. Do not let your hearts be troubled and do not be afraid"* (John 14:27 NIV).

To yield to Christ means that we open our heart, yield our will, and surrender ourselves into His arms of love, trusting that God is faithful to care for us, no matter what. Babies yield themselves when they fall asleep in their mother's arms. Lovers yield to each other's embrace. Yielding is a place of ultimate, total trust, rest, and loving assurance. When we relax our will and yield to Christ moment by moment, we let go of the need to control people or situations through our intellect or will. It's a lifestyle of radical trust.

Yielding feels a little bit like being so relaxed we could fall backward into someone's arms if we allowed ourselves to do so. With practice, we can gradually become a wholly yielded vessel, letting go of willpower, agendas, and self-assertion, open to the love and peace of God flowing in and through our spirit. This is what it means to practice the presence of God.

With practice, our perception of slight changes in the spiritual atmosphere can become finely tuned. We will begin to distinguish subtle movements of the Holy Spirit and notice that the presence of God feels stronger at certain times than at others. When we read the Bible, we may notice an increase in God's presence in our belly as we linger over certain verses. That means the Lord wants to speak to us through that particular Scripture.

The key is maintaining an awareness and yieldedness to God's Spirit within, then yielding more and more to Him. There is no end to the depths of just how surrendered we can be to the marvelous love of Christ within.

## THE FIVE GS OF PEACE

There are some helpful reminders we use when it comes to walking in the peace of God. For us, we came up with a list of five aspects of peace that all begin with the letter *G* so we can better teach and understand how the peace of God works in our hearts and our minds.

### Govern

The first aspect of peace is that it governs. When the peace of God governs us, we learn to walk in such a way that it rules our hearts and our minds. Paul wrote to the Colossians, telling them to let the peace of God govern their hearts. The Amplified Bible says it this way:

> *And let the peace (soul harmony which comes) from Christ rule (act as umpire continually) in your hearts [deciding and settling with finality all questions that arise in your minds, in that peaceful state] to which as [members of Christ's] one body you were also called [to live]. And be thankful (appreciative), [giving praise to God always]* (Colossians 3:15 AMP).

To umpire means that we let God call the shots in life. He gets to decide whether we're safe or whether we're out, whether it's a yes or it's a no. When the peace of God governs us, we let God guide us in our decision-making process, being the final authority on all matters related to life. His peace dictates when we move forward or when we move back, or whether or not we move at all. His peace continually acts as an umpire in every decision we make and every step that we take.

Dennis and I really believe that we're on the verge of seeing a revolution in the spiritual walk in the church. We are entering into the era of the God-emotions. They are going to rise up within us, and we'll be as easily able to tap into the fruit of the Spirit as we've been able to tap into the gifts of the Spirit, because it's going to be the character and the nature of God residing within us. God's peace is getting ready to come upon the church in unprecedented ways.

In our day-to-day routine, if we would just apply this principle of allowing God to rule within us, then we would be walking in the will of God because peace is ruling our hearts. Since He's the King and He's the One on the throne, the way to live our lives is by letting Him govern our hearts by His peace, thus including Him in all our circumstances.

## Guide

The second aspect of peace is that it guides. *"And let the peace (soul harmony which comes) from Christ rule (act as umpire continually) in your hearts"* (Col. 3:15 AMP) means that God gets to call the shots. Yes, He governs us by calling the shots, but that also means He guides us as well. Before we make a decision based strictly on the pros and cons of our intellect, we must let peace bear witness within and let it umpire and guide us in the decisions we face. If there's peace, then we can go ahead; if there's a red light (an internal loss of peace), then perhaps we should respect that and stop.

The way that works for us is like this: when we're thinking about a decision we have to make, something we need to be guided in, then we immediately focus on the peace within. If there is a feeling of anxiety, even if it's mild, it's a disturbance and not of God. Peace must rule within to guide us in whatever we do. A lack of peace is God's guidance as well.

We have to be neutral in obeying God if we expect peace to guide us. Some people say, "I want what I want, and I want it now!" And they say they have peace about it; but that is false peace. We can't desire to do something so badly that we want the peace to manifest—we must simply be neutral in obeying what God desires for us. We can't force the peace to be present, and we can't ignore it when it is not there.

When we're neutral to obey God, we simply have a heart to obey Him in whatever He tells us to do. And when we're neutral to the situation and we only want to obey God in whatever He wants, then peace can continually guide us. We lose our peace when the answer is a no. Even if it's a perception that we can't put our finger, we know it's the absence of peace, and God is saying no to that particular decision.

I (Dennis) once had a serious decision about moving to Charlotte, North Carolina. I had never been to Charlotte before, and God was giving me direction to go there. In my mind, of course, I questioned *because* I don't know anyone in Charlotte; I knew no logical reason to be there. As soon as I would drop down into my spirit and say, "But I want what God wants," the peace would come flooding into my heart. I knew beyond the shadow of a doubt that I was neutral about the decision, which was key for guidance to come. I had no predilection either way. I wanted what God wanted. And for guidance to be effective, that has to be the focus. And then I asked Him, "Should I leave for Charlotte now?" And the peace increased.

I have lived a lifestyle of communion with God long enough that trial and error has shown me walking in peace has been more reliable in my relationship with Christ than all of the natural information put together. If the peace guides me, then I know I'm in His will.

## *Guard*

The third aspect of peace is that it guards our heart and our mind. Philippians 4:7 says, *"And the peace of God, which surpasses all understanding, will guard your hearts and minds through Christ Jesus." Guard* means to keep us safe and secure in His presence regardless of external circumstances.

What Paul writes about peace wasn't meant to be poetry or fluffy words—it was meant to be an encounter with Christ. Peace guarding our heart was meant to be a supernatural experience—not a definition we memorized. For when peace guards our heart, we can be in any type of hostile environment and still perceive the exterior atmosphere but abide in peace within.

One time I (Dennis) was working in a halfway house of men that were getting out of prison. I inwardly had peace, but outwardly, from the place of peace, I discerned the atmosphere was suddenly charged, evil, and chaotic. Nothing was said in the natural, but it was usually the kind of feeling I would get when someone was going to make a break for it or do something crazy. The atmosphere suddenly shifted.

I was standing by one of the exit doors, when one of the men, who had failed to take his medication, pulled a knife and started to move toward me. He threatened me to move out of the way because he was making a break for it. And the supernatural peace of God made me feel safe and secure beyond my understanding, and I just knew that the peace was impenetrable. The man simply put the knife down and fell to his knees. What better place to possess peace than in a hostile environment like that.

### Gather

The fourth aspect of peace is that it gathers. It has a magnetic power to it. Abiding in Christ is something I've (Dennis) been walking in for quite some time now, and I've had people come up to me and just stand by me in order to feel God's peace. Even troubled congregation members will often come up and ask, "Is it okay if I just stand by you for a minute?" They want to experience the Prince of Peace, whom I carry with me every moment of every day.

Throughout my years of ministry, I've also had non-Christians come up to me and say, "I feel peace coming from you; I want that." It is a great tool for evangelism. I don't feel like I'm the most articulate person when it comes to evangelism, but I know one thing is that when they're attracted to the peace of God within me, I respond by telling them that Christ works from the inside out. I say, "You can have this same peace too. You're feeling it on the outside, but God can give it to you on the inside if you'll receive Him. Then you'll have peace with God."

We've even had unsaved people come up to us in the middle of the mall, just weeping for no reason whatsoever. It's because they feel the peace of God residing with us. The peace of God gathers others around us, giving them a sense of comfort and rest from turmoil surrounding them.

### *Ground*

The peace of God also grounds us in our daily lives. There are rich encounters we can have in God, and there is a progressive way of practicing His presence that grounds us in the reality of His peace. There are beautiful opportunities to impart and experience the peace of God, but the greatest truth is having it grounded and established in our hearts by practice.

We prayed for a woman at a meeting on the coast of North Carolina, asking God for an emotional healing directed toward forgiving her mother. She wept as we led her through prayer. And then she said, "I've been harboring this bitterness for far too long. And this is the first time I've ever felt peace in my life."

And then she later notified us that she had supernaturally lost around 100 pounds, and the weight was continuing to come off. People she didn't even know came up to her, saying, "I have clothes to give you." They supplied her with a new wardrobe in the process of all that was taking place—it was a double blessing. The peace of God grounded her, causing supernatural blessing to come to so many aspects of her life.

So God's peace roots us in reality, it roots us in the present. When we are living with the peace of God ruling and reigning in our life, we are living as people who are firmly planted, unshakable, and always abounding in the work of God. So peace governs, guides, guards, gathers, and grounds us in the love of God.

## Stuck in Traffic

When Jennifer and I minister, we always travel so that we go from church to church without much downtime in between. It was about 10 p.m., we had been driving for 13½ hours, and we were only one mile from the hotel we were going to stay at for the night. Suddenly the traffic came to a complete standstill. All eight lanes were blocked off and we watched as the police put up yellow crime scene tape.

Jennifer looked at me, and we were both thinking the same thing—*we were just one mile from a bed*. Our initial reaction was to become worried and move out of peace because of the circumstances. But we said, "No, we're going to practice what we preach." So we just closed our eyes right there in the car and yielded to the peace within.

We basically said to ourselves, "This place of peace is where we live. This is where we've learned everything. We're not going to get involved in this. We're going to Him." And when we dropped down and allowed the peace to rule, even though our head had not a clue as to what was going to transpire, an abiding peace invaded our hearts.

I felt led to move one car length over, which is ridiculous with hundreds of stalled cars all around us. I didn't think, *I think I'm going to change lanes*. I was paying more attention to my gut than my head. I wasn't looking for a second opinion—I was looking for God's opinion.

We were near the tape when I pulled the car into the other lane. Almost immediately a policeman came and pulled back the tape, and eight or nine cars were let through, then he put the tape back, stopping traffic once again. Our car was the last one to go through. We read in the paper and heard on the news the following day that the highway was closed until 6 A.M. because the police were looking for shell casings from a shootout involving the police.

It was such a supernatural event. We believe the officer was an angel that let us through that night. But we honored

God in the midst of what seemed to be contrary circumstances. When we chose to drop down into the peace of God, we were essentially saying, "I want Your rule regardless of the circumstances." And in honoring Him, God says, *"For those who honor Me I will honor, and those who despise Me shall be lightly esteemed"* (1 Sam. 2:30).

This same peace can affect the lives of anyone who will yield to Him.

# COMMUNION WITHOUT CEASING

If our thoughts turn to worries and fears, our attention and affections drift away from Christ, and we are no longer focused on our spirit. We will no longer feel the peace of God reigning within. As soon as we notice we are not feeling peace, then we can drop down and return to Christ within.

## Practice

*Place your hand on your belly to help you focus. Sit down, close your eyes, and imagine that door opening in your belly as you relax your will. Inside, you should feel open. This is what it feels like to yield your heart to the Lord. His presence and His peace will flood your heart.*

*Now think of a concern, offense, or worry, or picture someone who hurt you. Notice that you feel God's peace diminish and stress return. Drop down again and yield your will. Release any troubling concern into the hands of God. His presence and His peace will return without fail.*

It's a simple formula: if we drop down and yield to Christ, we will experience the peace of God. But if we're living in our head or through our carnal emotions, we will live in an under-current of mild to strong anxiety when negative thoughts or emotions arise. It is important we notice the difference between yielding and not yielding our heart to Christ.

This may be wonderful in theory, but you may say, "The emotional pain and negative thoughts bombard me throughout the day! How can I abide in Christ when I can barely function?"

This is the marvelous secret of supernatural forgiveness, an easy 1-2-3 process to release Christ the forgiver, explained in the next chapter. It is not a method any more than the Romans Road to salvation is a method. It is only an explana-tion of a spiritual process that demystifies a walk in the Spirit.

## FORGIVE 1-2-3

One definition of *prayer* is "spiritual communion." Another way to think of communion is heart connection.

When we are really involved with another person relationally, we genuinely care for them and care about them—our hearts become *knit* together. Mothers *bond* with babies. Lovers *bond* in marriage. And God wants to bond with us, spirit to Spirit, heart to heart.

But there are often roadblocks along the way on our part. The Bible says that we have the ability to open and shut the door to our hearts. The apostle John asks, *"Whoever has this world's goods, and sees his brother in need, and shuts up his heart from him, how does the love of God abide in him?"* (1 John 3:17).

But as long as the door of our heart is open to God, we can experience His presence. If we are worried, stressed, angry, or preoccupied with the cares of life, however, we have closed the door of our heart with our will, and we will no longer experience His presence. He hasn't moved away, we have!

In both the Old and New Testaments, the Lord promises that *"He will not leave you nor forsake you"* (Deut. 31:6; Heb. 13:5), but we can lose our Christ-awareness temporarily. If we move away from our spirit and focus on fears and worries, we will no longer experience His presence, although He is still near. We are simply choosing, by our will, to rely on our own strength and go at it alone. The alternative to relying on ourselves is to yield our will, open the door of our heart, and choose to abide in Christ within.

## FIRST, FEEL, FORGIVE

The three simple steps to abiding in Christ without ceasing: first-feel-forgive. If we follow this 1-2-3 process, we will be healed and made emotionally whole in a very short time—and remain healed. We'll carry the peace, love, and joy of the Lord wherever we go, sharing God's manifest presence with the hurting and lost rather than just trying to keep our own head above water, out of stress, worry, and despair.

Too many people are afraid of their emotions. They hide them behind masks, deny them, suppress them, or try to numb them with drugs or alcohol. Those are merely Band-Aid solutions. Negative emotions are not something to fear, but are simply a temporary interruption to peace. Forgiveness is the fast, permanent solution.

Whenever we experience forgiveness, it will wash away barriers, and peace will be restored instantly. Forgiveness always works to get our peace back. Few things are 100 percent guaranteed, but forgiveness is one of those things. It is the never-fail solution.

## READY TO BE FREE?

We promise that this process will work for you, no matter how deep and longstanding your emotional pain. These three easy steps came from our observations about how the Holy Spirit ministers healing to individuals. We simply allowed the Holy Spirit freedom to minister, and we facilitated by following His lead, later documenting what God taught us. These steps have proven to be ultra-effective over decades. We have never been disappointed: the Lord Himself has shown us that He *never* refuses to cleanse a heart that is filled with pain. All we have to do is present the pain to Him, yield, and allow His forgiveness to wash away any toxic emotions. Freedom is that easy.

First, get comfortable. Find a quiet place to sit alone with God, without the distractions of cell phones, e-mails, friends, or family. This is your time to meet with the Lord. He longs to meet with you—and is already closer than your breath. It helps to close your eyes and put your hand on your belly, the location of your heart. Now drop down and focus on Christ within. Open the door of your will and yield to God. By dropping down and opening up to Christ, you are inviting Him to work in you.

You're ready to begin Forgive 1-2-3.

Chapter 9

# FORGIVE 1-2-3

## 1. FIRST

This is where we invite the Lord to bring to mind some circumstance or relationship where there is a need of healing. Focus on the first person or situation that comes to mind. You may see a picture in your mind's eye or a short "movie clip" of a moment in the present or past.

Don't dismiss or overlook any picture or memory that seems insignificant or random. God knows what is important—and also knows the best order in which to proceed in the process of healing. Most often, the issues that seem small to us have tremendous significance in our lives. God always knows best. Trust Him to bring to mind whatever He feels is most important to heal first.

It may help to think of yourself as a child who needs help. So go to your heavenly Father with childlike faith, simply trusting that the first person or situation that comes to mind is truly from an all-knowing, all-loving God, who is powerful enough to communicate with you clearly and directly.

## 2. FEEL

Next, we get in touch with the feelings that are taking place in our gut. "What do I feel when I think of or imagine this person or situation that just came to mind?" Every thought has a corresponding emotion. All thoughts are feeling-thoughts or emo-cognitions.

Pay attention to the negative emotions you feel in your belly area. Don't think at this point, but simply feel what is taking place in your gut. When you think of that person or situation that God brings to mind, what is going on inside your belly?

We don't even have to name the emotion we are currently experiencing. It may be very subtle or extremely strong, from a vague, nameless discomfort to a more obvious rage or sorrow. We only have to feel the negative emotion momentarily. God does not require us to feel the full extent of our emotions in order to receive healing. There is no reason for us to dwell on the feeling or plumb its depths. Just experiencing "the tip of the iceberg" of an enormous feeling is sufficient—no more.

What if feeling a particularly painful emotion seems more than you can handle at the moment? Just remind yourself that feeling a moment of discomfort is a small price to pay for a lifetime of peace and freedom in that area. Give in and allow the feelings to arise. Christ can work with whatever area of brokenness you offer Him, no matter how small, confused, painful, or undefined. All you need is a mustard seed of faith.

As we think of the person or situation God brings to mind, what does it feel like inside of us? That emotion has been in us all along, even if it was hidden. But it has been lurking beneath our conscious awareness. Unresolved emotions are stored in the brain's long-term memory, in the cellular memories of the body, and the emotional memory of the heart but God will bring to the surface what He wants to heal, and He'll do it in the best order possible. He has our best interests at heart.

### 3. FORGIVE

It is important to always start with the emotion that we're feeling. While we continue to feel that particular emotion, drop down to focus on our spirit and yield our will to God, opening the door of our heart to the presence of God. Yield to Christ within, and allow a river of forgiveness to flow toward the person who provoked the negative emotion (or we receive forgiveness for ourselves).

Forgiveness is complete when the negative emotion changes to perfect peace. Christ Himself will bring healing to the wound in our heart—and to our cellular memories and neural pathways—with His very presence, giving us peace that transcends understanding.

Forgiveness flowing from our innermost being actually feels like a gentle river of love rushing from inside our belly out toward the person needing forgiveness or the situation the Lord wants to heal. Let His river flow until the pain, fear, or anger changes to peace. Then and only then has that unforgiveness been cleansed by Christ Himself. In fact, that's the sign of forgiveness: pain has changed to His peace.

The most important question is whether or not we feel peace inside when we think of the person or situation again. We never have to guess if we did it right if we focus on the peace. We can just close our eyes, drop down, picture the exact situation or person again, and we should now feel peace—a permanent and lasting peace. If we can see that person who offended us or return to the memory and feel peace instead of pain or bitterness, then forgiveness is complete.

If, on the other hand, we picture the person or situation and feel even a twinge of negative emotion, then we need to return to the process of dropping down, yielding our will, and releasing Christ the forgiver once again. It's imperative we keep releasing love until the emotion turns to peace.

Christ the forgiver is the One who does the forgiving. There is nothing for us to do but yield to Him and let His river of love flow through us. It should only take seconds.

It is extremely important that we pray through only one situation at a time, and pray through each emotion associated with that memory, releasing Christ the forgiver until we feel His peace displace the negative emotion. We must be patient with whatever God presents to us, in whatever order, no matter how "random" it seems.

Sequence is important, so we always go in God's order, according to His leading. He is aware of the larger structures of our soul and understands how to dismantle strongholds, wound by wound, in the most effective sequence.

### Forgive in Three Directions

Often we have to forgive in more than one direction. Forgiveness may be directed toward another person or situation, but it can also be directed toward God or ourselves. Why? Perhaps we've held onto regrets from the past or held judgments against others. We need to let Christ cleanse us of those regrets and accusations. When we hold onto unforgiveness, it's a sin.

Maybe we feel guilt and shame about things we've done or haven't done, sins of omission or commission. We simply open our heart, yield our will, and let Christ the forgiver flow toward us, cleansing us of sin. We need to forgive ourselves for judging ourselves too harshly. People are frequently much harder on themselves than on other people.

But sometimes we need to forgive God—not that He has done anything wrong, but we blame Him for things done to us. Even though He has never done anything wrong or sinned in any way, people often get mad at Him anyway. He's accused of withholding blessings from us, or maybe we've grown bitter and disappointed by hopes that were deferred. Once again, we open our heart and yield our will to Christ. We allow forgiveness to flow out, toward God Himself. We also receive forgiveness for holding a grudge against the Lord. Forgiving God gets our heart right toward Him.

At other times we need to forgive others for what has been done to us. A person who was abused, for example, might be angry with the perpetrator, blame themselves for not stopping it somehow, and feel hurt by God because it was allowed to happen. That person can open their heart, yield their will, and let the forgiveness of Christ flow in all three directions—first to the perpetrator, then to themselves, and then to God. If in doubt, we should forgive in all three directions because we can't forgive too much or love too much.

### *Authority to Rule*

One of the unique aspects about this approach is that it always deals with the emotions first. Whenever we experience a negative emotion, Christ is not the authority in our heart at that particular moment. When peace rules our heart, then it is Christ Himself ruling our heart. Remember Paul's admonition: *"Let the peace of God rule in your hearts"* (Col. 3:15).

So a believer's authority comes through the rule and reign of Christ. All authority comes from the ruling presence of Jesus over the human heart. When Jesus is ruling in our hearts through peace, His presence then guards our hearts: *"The peace of God, which surpasses understanding, will guard your hearts and minds through Christ Jesus"* (Phil. 4:7).

So we must deal with any negative emotion through forgiveness first, and then we will have the authority to deal with the thoughts and mental strongholds that cloud up our thinking.

## 4. FACT

Most of the time there is no lie, or stronghold, that needs to come down. Lies come in at the time of emotional wounding, but the vast majority of emotional wounds do not have a lie attached to them. In Dennis's and my experience, only about one out of every 30 or 40 emotional healings has a lie attached to it. Therefore, we *always* start with the emotion. When we deal with a negative emotion through forgiveness and receive peace, we have the spiritual authority to deal with that lie. Peace is the place of power.

After releasing forgiveness, if there is a lie attached, it will immediately come to mind. We don't have to guess, search for it, or analyze what is taking place in order to find it. We will just know because it will pop into our mind.

Now that we are experiencing God's *shalom* and receiving His revealed truth, we are in the place of spiritual power to pull down strongholds in the name of the God of peace: *"the God of peace shall crush satan under your feet shortly"* (Rom. 16:20). Spiritual warfare and intercession done from the place of peace through the Prince of Peace are infinitely more powerful and effective than contending and striving in prayer with an anxious, troubled spirit.

Verbally renounce any lie that contradicts God's Word or His loving nature, yield once more, and let Christ the forgiver flow into your innermost being. Now wait, and allow the Lord to show you the truth: "What do You say, Lord?"

A Scripture or scriptural phrase will come to mind immediately. Receive God's truth and then say the truth out loud. Factual truth will replace the lie that has been a stronghold for years. It is important we write it in our journal so we can remember what He did. And then we use the facts spoken to our heart by the Lord to declare God's truth about ourselves, our situation, or another person.

We receive God's truth with gratitude and cherish His Word in our heart and soul. Then we allow Him to write it on the tablet of our heart. In this way, we are then able to cast down strongholds *"and every high thing that exalts itself against the knowledge of God"* (2 Cor. 10:5).

## 5. FILL

If a lie came to mind, deal with that. If we have an emotional need that wasn't met in childhood—for example, love, attention, or approval—then we must forgive the person who didn't give us what we needed, and release the internal demand to get that need filled by anyone or anything other than God. Then welcome Him to fill that area of need with His love.

Simply drop down, yield your will, and open your heart to receive more of Him. He longs to fill His children with His overflowing, overwhelming love. This is the goal of all forgiveness: to be filled with Christ Himself. It is our Father's good pleasure to give us His kingdom of righteousness, peace, and joy within (see Luke 12:32).

God created us to need love, nurture, and affirmation. But God also knows that parents are not perfect, so He promised to take care of the deficiencies they left us with. God delights in filling His children's hearts with what they need. He can give us what no earthly parent could ever supply. David said, *"When my father and my mother forsake me, then the Lord will take care of me"* (Ps. 27:10).

All children need the comfort and care of their parents. These needs are legitimate and given by God. But God has also made provision to comfort and care for us even when our parents let us down:

*Blessed be the God and Father of our Lord Jesus Christ, the Father of mercies and God of all comfort, who comforts us in all our tribulation, that we may be able to comfort those who are in any trouble, with the comfort with which we ourselves are comforted by God. For as the sufferings of Christ abound in us, so our consolation also abounds through Christ* (2 Corinthians 1:3-5).

## THE FORGIVENESS LIFESTYLE

This process of first-feel-forgive is a fast and effective God encounter that we can have multiple times every hour of every day. This is what we describe as "the forgiveness lifestyle."

Throughout the day, practice the presence of God by dropping down, yielding your will to God, remaining open in your heart, and basking in the peace of Christ. The moment any negative emotion disturbs your peace, you can begin the first-feel-forgive process. Forgiveness will become a habit of being, a lifestyle that is practiced in order to commune with Christ without ceasing.

Notice any overreaction you have toward a person or circumstance. There is usually some deeper issue involved. You don't have to try to figure out where the overreaction came from. When there is adequate time, ask the Lord to show you the source of any negative emotion. "Where did it get started, Lord?" Begin with the first person or situation that comes to mind; feel the feeling associated with that memory;

and then forgive by yielding to Christ the forgiver as He flows to and through that person and situation to bring forgiveness and healing where there was wounding and offense.

It's that simple: *first-feel-forgive* throughout the day. With practice, we can begin to abide in Christ. As each negative feeling interrupts our *shalom,* we yield our will to Christ and allow Him to do the rest.

Experiencing supernatural forgiveness is vital to our everyday life—no matter the context or occasion. Drop down to stay in peace, for example, with our family at the holidays. We don't have to lose our peace when we're caught in a traffic jam or stuck in a long grocery line, or busily making dinner, doing homework, or attending a business lunch.

Jake's boss was yelling at him, blaming him for something his coworker had done. Jake simply dropped down, yielded his will to God, released forgiveness to his boss, and immediately experienced God's peace and allowed the love of Christ to flow. His coworker later went to the boss and confessed what he had done.

A pastor was waiting in line at the grocery store with a "crabby clerk," keeping everyone waiting. The pastor simply dropped down, yielded his will, and allowed Christ's love to flow to the clerk. He experienced God's marvelous peace while the other customers were getting upset. Even more exciting was that by the time he made his purchase, the clerk was actually beginning to smile.

## REVIEW

Once again, just follow these easy steps to experience supernatural forgiveness:

### *First*

*First person or situation. What is the first person or situation God brings to mind in an image or memory?*

### *Feel*

*Feel the feeling. What is the emotion you feel in your gut?*

### *Forgive*

*Forgive. Yield your will and let Christ the forgiver flow out toward the person or situation, yourself, or to God.*

### *Fact*

*Fact. After forgiving and getting peace, if there is a lie, renounce it out loud. Next, ask the Lord for the truth (scriptural fact) and receive it.*

### *Fill*

*Fill. Forgive first, then release the demands on people to give you what you needed. Then receive filling from Christ within.*

Be mindful that these simple steps contradict the most common misconceptions about forgiveness: Christ is the forgiver, so forgiveness works every time; forgiveness is instantaneous, not a process; there are no small or large offenses, all forgiveness is easy for Jesus to accomplish. Now we're going to talk about staying connected 24/7.

Chapter 10

# STAY CONNECTED 24/7

## CONNECTED 24/7

Communion with Christ can be enjoyed by simply maintaining our connection with God. We start by making a connection in prayer, and then practice connecting in everyday life. Start connected, stay connected.

Picture getting married to someone you truly loved for much of your life. You finally are married, the longing and anticipation to be with one another is finally over. You live together now, but you only let them in the door for ten minutes, twice a day. They stand there on the front porch, patiently waiting all day and all night—but you just ignore them until it is convenient for you. Who would tolerate a marriage like that? We know we wouldn't. That is not a relationship at all.

Communing with someone is enjoying a real relationship with him or her. When you commune, you share each other's thoughts and feelings in a profoundly close relationship. Communion is based on deep intimacy, vulnerability, and transparency, sharing your being with another without restraint, fear, or shame.

In John 15, Jesus invites us to abide in Him and stay connected with Him all the time. Communion with God is touching His presence within our spirit—and yielding to Christ the forgiver as soon as anything interrupts our peace.

In the Gospels, we learn that Jesus chose to be alone for prayer at times, but we also learn that He was in continuous fellowship with the Father, maintaining a spiritual connection with God in the middle of jostling crowds in the noisy marketplace. He had set times of prayer, yes, but He also abided in the Father.

> *Then Jesus answered and said to them, "Most assuredly, I say to you, the Son can do nothing of Himself, but what He sees the Father do..."* (John 5:19).

The apostle John also gives us the wonderful news that we, too, can have that same intimate communion with God. John enjoyed a relationship with Jesus during His time on earth, but he also writes that he was still having fellowship with Him after Jesus's death, resurrection, and ascension. And that same communion is available for all believers alive on the earth today:

> *The infinite Life of God Himself took shape before us. We saw it, we heard it, and now we're telling you so you can experience it along with us, this experience of communion with the Father and His Son, Jesus Christ* (1 John 1:2-3 MSG).

We may not talk to God continuously, but we can learn to touch His presence, spirit to Spirit, without interruption every moment of every day. It is truly possible to *"pray without ceasing"* (1 Thess. 5:17) when we understand prayer in terms of abiding rather than asking for things.

We can experience union with God throughout the day, but especially during our devotional time, as we focus only on Him, one on One, face to face. To stay connected during the day, it is vital to start the day connected by having a morning devotional time. Then, the second key is to pay attention to our emotions throughout the day. If we lose our peace, then we practice forgiveness and we'll get our peace back almost immediately. If we're going to learn something new, it will take some practice to make it part of our lifestyle.

## SIMPLE PRAYER

Prayer should be simple—easy, uncomplicated, no mixture, undefiled, complete; nothing extra, nothing missing. Pure is a synonym of simple. Simple prayer is prayer focused on God alone, prayer that is pure, with only one aim: to adore and glorify God.

Prayer is nothing more than spending a special time in the presence of God. It is not necessarily talking and rattling off a list of things we want God to do for us, although it can include that. But more than anything, prayer is about connecting with God in an intimate way.

Paul wrote to the Corinthian church:

> For I am jealous for you with a godly jealousy; for I betrothed you to one husband, so that to Christ I might present you as a pure virgin. But I am afraid that, as the serpent deceived Eve by his craftiness, your minds will be led astray from the simplicity and purity of devotion to Christ (2 Corinthians 11:2-3 NASB).

When we devote time to communing with God, then we come before the Lord expecting to meet with Him and touch His presence. This is a devoted time, an offering of our time given as a holy gift to God. We present ourselves to Him and yield our will. We drop down to our spirit and open the door of our heart. We are coming before God to honor and love Him, so we must dedicate ourselves to Him as a living sacrifice.

Consider this time as time to seek God for Himself alone. Make God your number one priority. This is not the time to petition for your own needs or to intercede on behalf of others, although petitions and intercession are certainly important. The attitude of your heart is focused on pursuing a loving friendship with God. This time of profound communion is the good soil where deep intimacy begins to grow.

## WHAT IS SIMPLE PRAYER?

"Simple prayer" is one of several terms that are used to describe prayer in which a person waits quietly before the Lord. Perhaps the best word to describe simple prayer would be *abiding*.

In John 15, Jesus tells us to abide in Him, and He gives us the metaphor of the vine and the branches. A branch must be connected to its life source, the vine, to be able to flourish and produce fruit. In the same way, a believer walks in the Spirit by maintaining a spiritual connection with God. Jesus said,

> *Abide in Me, and I in you. As the branch cannot bear fruit of itself, unless it abides in the vine, neither can you, unless you abide in Me.*

> *I am the vine, you are the branches. He who*
> *abides in Me, and I in him, bears much fruit; for*
> *without Me you can do nothing.... By this My*
> *Father is glorified, that you bear much fruit; so*
> *you will be My disciples* (John 15:4-5,8).

As we wait silently, without speaking, we simply become aware of the presence of the Lord in our heart. This way of prayer is both a relationship with God and a discipline that encourages growth of the relationship.

Simple prayer is not intended to replace other types of prayer. However, it does bring deeper meaning to all prayer and leads us from more active kinds of prayer into prayer in which we abide in God and commune with Him. The psalmist said, *"Surely I have calmed and quieted my soul, like a weaned child with his mother; like a weaned child is my soul within me"* (Ps. 131:2).

And Zephaniah declared:

> *The Lord your God in your midst, The Mighty*
> *One, will save; He will rejoice over you with glad-*
> *ness, He will quiet you with His love, He will*
> *rejoice over you with singing* (Zephaniah 3:17).

The two necessary ingredients of abiding prayer are silence and stillness. If we have ever stilled our thoughts in our prayer time or church to quietly enjoy God's presence, we have already experienced silent prayer. The mind does not become blank, but awareness of God's presence and peace increases. We must have silence and stillness if we are to grow in relationship and communion with God.

## A PRACTICAL PLAN

Remember that we are spending time with a Person—we are being with Jesus. When we set apart time to spend alone communing with Jesus, we honor God and attract His attention. Most people never get around to a prayer time unless they actually make some kind of plan beforehand. We will never know if we're failing in a particular area if we don't have a plan to measure our success by.

It is important to decide on a time to pray. If we don't devote a specific prayer time into our schedule, it is too easy to skip it. It is best to decide the time the night before so we can get the needed rest and be able to be refreshed and focused when we enter the time of prayer. It is also important to find a quiet place with a comfortable chair. If we're distracted by all the noise around us, or if we're not comfortable, those are things that will distract us from completely focusing on Him.

A Bible, a pen or pencil, and a journal are good so that we can keep a written record of what God is impressing upon our heart or speaking to us about. Many people have asked us how long they should spend in prayer. We suggest, if just starting out, to spend a minimum of 20–30 minutes in prayer each day. We suggest this because it is enough time for our flesh to quiet itself in the presence of God, stilling our thoughts. When we feel peace, we will lose the urge to do something other than pray (see Ps. 131:2; Isa. 40:31). This is a good time frame that can be used as a launching board to spend more time with God.

During this time, drop down, focus on Christ, and allow His presence to flood your mind, will, and emotions. As you do, expect the surroundings to slip away and to be so caught up with Him that you may lose your sense of time, even though you may feel some initial resistance from your flesh. This resistance will fade as you say no to distractions and stretch your capacity to remain in His presence. Small victories develop power to overcome the flesh.

## DAILY PRAYER

As the Lord gives His attention to us, we also acknowledge Him as a real Person with us. We come before Him in reverence (see Heb. 4:13) because we have an audience with the King of kings! When we present ourselves to the Lord, know that He is giving us His undivided attention. We are His constant delight. Every time we draw close to Him, we ravish His heart. Because of this, we should honor Him with humility and in adoration as His servant.

Awareness of the Lord and sensitivity to His presence are progressive and are based on the discovery of who God is. We take the posture of a student before the Master Teacher—we don't have anything to say until we have heard from Him (see Isa. 50:4).

The Holy Spirit may speak through whispers, impressions, pictures, or through Scripture. Be patient. Just as natural growth takes time, spiritual growth needs time to develop as well (see Ps. 27:14). As you become accustomed to being still before the Lord, you will be able to stay in prayer for longer periods of time.

The Lord will bring any sins to your remembrance with a very gentle, loving nudge of His Spirit. His voice is never condemning or judgmental. If you hear an accusing, harsh voice in your thoughts, be assured that it is the enemy's voice sent to discourage you.

It is the goodness of the Lord that leads us to repentance (see Rom. 2:4). If He does bring sins to our mind, then we yield our will and receive forgiveness, opening our heart to the *"washing of the water by the word"* (Eph. 5:26; see also Titus 3:5). So welcome a fresh touch, a cleansing, and refreshing from the Holy Spirit.

## FRIENDSHIP WITH GOD

Time spent in prayer prepares us to walk as a friend of God during the day. A parent helps a child get ready for new adventures, gives him or her much-needed words of wisdom, and provides loving support. Our heavenly Father knows what we will face each day and desires to give us everything we need to successfully navigate through life. But even more than that, He will be right there with us every step of the way.

Friends genuinely care about one another. Since God has emotions just like we do, He can rejoice and laugh; He celebrates the prodigal and grieves for the sinner. He is a deeply emotional Person. Nothing is more amazing or necessary in life than to intimately know this emotional, brilliant, ecstatically loving God. He is Love Himself. He loves you, and He wants you to love Him in return.

Communion with Love Himself is not a special gift for certain saints or hidden knowledge for experts. Any believer, young or old, is meant to experience oneness with the Beloved.

The Lord Jesus Christ took our sins upon Himself on the cross and rose again in victory for this unspeakably glorious access to His presence. We are the "bride" of the Lamb (see Rev. 21:9). Jesus also said, *"I have called you friends"* (John 15:15).

Experiencing God as a friend is different from doing good works or making great sacrifices. It is touching His presence continually, without the interference of the enemy's inroads of fear, stress, or anxiety. Friendship with God is learning to abide in Christ without ceasing.

When God called Abraham his friend in Second Chronicles 20:7 and Isaiah 41:8, the Hebrew word used is *ahab*. This same Hebrew word is also translated "lover" or "one who is loving and beloved, intimate; different from a companion." This Hebrew term *ahab* also means "to desire, to breathe after." Imagine this intimate "breathing after" that described Abraham's friendship with God.

Moses was also called a friend of God (see Exod. 33:11), but the Hebrew term used in this passage is *rea'*, translated as "companion" or "neighbor." Moses was a neighbor or companion of God, whereas Abraham was God's beloved, His intimate one. Abraham had a deeper degree of intimacy with God than Moses had.

Because of the cross, our degree of intimacy with God is even greater than Abraham's. Unlike Abraham, we have the Spirit of Christ living within us. Before the cross, the Holy Spirit could not dwell within believers. But now, because of the glorious cross and resurrection, we are one with Christ.

The Lord's invitation to His followers is simple and clear: *"Abide in Me, and I in you"* (John 15:4). With consistent and diligent practice, we can learn to experience His mind with our thoughts; we can experience His emotions with the emotions we feel; and we can encounter His dominion, His kingdom, with the actions we will to do, in perfect harmony with His will. We can learn to become wholly yielded vessels of love.

This is true friendship with God, the bliss of touching His presence with every breath we breathe.

# About the Authors

As a pastor and church planter, Dennis Clark has been in ministry for more than 30 years. Dr. Jennifer Clark holds a ThD in theology and BS, MS, EdS degrees in psychology and co-pastors with Dennis. They minister together full-time as a husband and wife team.

Dennis and Dr. Jen have developed simple, systematic, and proven how-to tools to set people free from emotional pain and equip them to teach it to others. They provide simple keys easy enough for a mom or Sunday school worker to teach a 3-year-old child, yet effective enough to heal the deepest hurts of adults quickly and completely.

The Clarks founded Full Stature Ministries and Kingdom Life Church, located in Fort Mill, South Carolina. They also direct TEAM Embassy, a Training Embassy for Advanced Ministry.

For video demonstrations and further teachings, visit:

www.forgive123.com

www.kingdomlifechurch.us

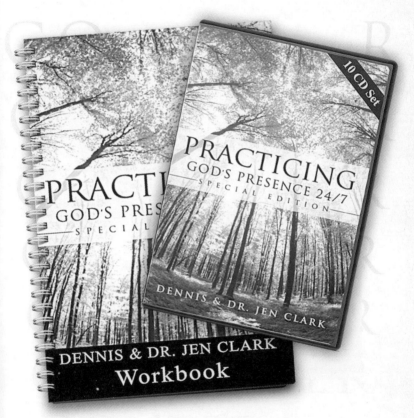

# Go Deeper